DOING THEOLOGY

with Huck & Jim

Parables for Understanding Doctrine

MARK SHAW

with questions for individuals
or for group discussion

INTERVARSITY PRESS
DOWNERS GROVE, ILLINOIS 60515

InterVarsity Press® is the book-publishing division of InterVarsity Christian Fellowship®, a student movement active on campus at hundreds of universities, colleges and schools of nursing in the United States of America, and a member movement of the International Fellowship of Evangelical Students. For information about local and regional activities, write Public Relations Dept., InterVarsity Christian Fellowship, 6400 Schroeder Rd., P.O. Box 7895, Madison, WI 53707-7895.

All Scripture quotations, unless otherwise indicated, are taken from the HOLY BIBLE, NEW INTERNA-TIONAL VERSION®. NIV®. Copyright ©1973, 1978, 1984 by International Bible Society. Used by permission of Zondervan Publishing House. All rights reserved.

Cover illustration: Brad Purse

ISBN 0-8308-1654-2

Printed in the United States of America ∞

Library of Congress Cataloging-in-Publication Data

Shaw, Mark, 1949-
    Doing theology with Huck and Jim: parables for understanding
    doctrine: with questions for individuals or for group discussion/
    Mark Shaw.
        p.   cm.
    Includes bibliographical references.
    ISBN 0-8308-1654-2 (alk. paper)
    1. Theology, Doctrinal—Popular works.   2. Storytelling—Religious
    aspects—Christianity.   3. Parables.   I. Title.
    BT77.S513   1993
    230—dc20   93-36209
                                                                                      CIP

| 15 | 14 | 13 | 12 | 11 | 10 | 9 | 8 | 7 | 6 | 5 | 4 | 3 | 2 |
| 04 | 03 | 02 | 01 | 00 | 99 | 98 | 97 | 96 | 95 | 94 | | | |

To Lois
Bibi yangu, rafiki yangu, upendo yangu

Introduction

In which the author introduces Huck and Jim, makes a confession, and offers some advice on how to use this book.

A full moon hung low on the river as Huck and Jim pulled the raft out of the weeds. They threw their bedrolls onto the wet surface of the raft, shimmering in the silver light. Huck could feel the cool Mississippi mud squeezing up between his toes as he pushed the raft out toward the current of the river. The mud felt good. Didn't feel like mud to him. Felt like freedom. No more church clothes. No more pinching shoes. No more books.

Huck and Jim jumped onto the raft and poled their way out into the silver-streaked darkness of the river. Huck looked back at the rooftops and steeples of the town outlined in moonlight. They were leaving it all behind—leaving it for good as far as he was concerned. He looked over at Jim and saw that Jim was looking back too. Then their eyes met and they started to smile at one another.

"No mo' sass from the white folk," said Jim, his big grin splitting the night.

"No more rules to keep," said Huck, grinning back, big as Jim's.

"No mo' looking down at my feet when I walk," Jim said, starting to laugh.

"No more looking out for the razor strap," Huck said, giggling.

"No mo' 'Jim do this' and 'Jim do that,' " Jim added, laughing harder now.

"No more books," Huck said, his hoots echoing off the stillness of the river bank.

Jim smiled at Huck's last statement but the smile was weak. Jim went silent and the conversation died in the coolness of the night and the gurgle of the river.

After a time Huck spoke up. "What'd you bring for food? I'm hungry."

Jim unwrapped his bedroll. His worldly wealth was contained in it. Immediately it was all laid out in full view. There was a hat and some fruit, a pair of socks, a rabbit's foot and a book. Jim tossed Huck a piece of fruit.

"What'd you bring a book for?" asked Huck with a tone of irritation.

"T' read," said Jim, rolling up the blanket again. "What else a book good for?"

"Didn't think you could read," Huck said and then wished he hadn't.

"I can read," Jim responded with intense seriousness, gazing into the night.

"What kinda book is it?" Huck asked.

"Book 'bout theology," Jim said, his voice trailing away.

"Theology! I hate theology almost as much as I hate schools and rules," Huck said, and emphasized the point by spitting into the river. "What good is a theology book on a trip like this?"

Jim was silent for a long time before he answered. "Trip like this is long. Lotta things gonna happen. Might come in handy."

Then Jim grabbed a pole, got up and pushed the raft through the moonbeams and out closer to the swift current that would take them downriver and closer to freedom.

The Theology Behind the Story: Understanding Theology

So Huck hates theology. I must confess that I feel some empathy with Huck on that point. I used to hate theology too. After I became a Christian my interest was in the Bible—not theology. I wanted vital experiences with the person of God, not stilted logical propositions about the concept of God. Even when I went to college and took theology courses, my class notes were as often filled with doodles as words. God and the Bible were in. Theology was out.

Then something happened. As I grew in my Christian faith, my longing to know God increased. My hunger to mine the gold in Scripture grew stronger. I was a pilgrim on a quest for more of God. I discovered that I needed maps of the routes that would take me to a deeper experience of the Bible and of the God of the Bible. I discovered that the maps were called theology. My naive rejection of theology was supplanted by my need to know God. My hunger to use theology as an aid to my spiritual pilgrimage grew. Systematic theology, biblical theology, historical theology—these became a growing interest for this pilgrim. I fell in love with theology.

After finishing graduate school I found myself teaching theology both in America and Africa. In my teaching I found students with a variety of reactions to theology.

I found some who reminded me of myself. They wanted God. They wanted the Bible. But they didn't necessarily want theology.

On the other hand, I found another kind of student who enjoyed theology as an intellectual challenge but saw very little connection between theology and the worship and enjoyment of God. I wanted very much to show both groups the maps that had led me to greater joy and satisfaction in God, but I couldn't seem to find the key. In desperation I began using stories to go along with my systematic theology lectures. The stories were often (but not always) based on childhood classics or fiction from popular culture. Some of the stories were takeoffs on fairy tales. Others were about characters like Huck Finn or Ebenezer Scrooge. There were tales inspired by detective stories, medieval legends, childhood classics, and modern fiction. We would discuss the stories and analyze them using Scripture, creeds and classic theological texts.

For those who had an allergy to theology, the stories seemed to bring the sneezing to a stop. For those who saw theology largely in cold, intellectual terms, the stories seemed to thaw some of the frost and create some new longings.

The method that I was employing to teach my students theology was hardly original. Christ had used parables to teach theological truths. C. S. Lewis was well known for teaching biblical truths in story form. American academic discussion of the use of narrative in communicating theology had gone on since H. Richard Niebuhr of Yale had broached the subject in the 1940s.

I will be using the narrative approach in this book. This is how I proceed: After I tell the story, I offer some theological commentary. The "Theology Behind the Story" section seeks to explain and analyze the parable. But it does more than that. It also provides a fuller exploration of the doctrine under consideration within the parable. Discussion questions on both the parable and commentary conclude each chapter.

What are some benefits of this method of study? One benefit is that the cherished truths of Scripture bloom with freshness when presented in story form rather than merely in theological propositions. Secondly, it seems ideally suited to the central task of theology—glorifying God by enjoying him. God is to be appreciated, not just studied. By combining story with scriptural and theological comment, it offers the benefits of the appeal to the imagination without sacrificing the propositional statements from which orthodox theology has historically been fashioned. By appealing to the imagination, this approach helps God's beauty and delightfulness shine through theological truths.

A third benefit is that it has the potential to take biblical truths to the heart of value systems or worldviews. Traditional ways of doing theology so focus on the intellectual understanding of various doctrines that sometimes the heart and imagination are left untouched. This approach seeks to penetrate to the basic beliefs that shape our behavior and form our character. Where do the basic beliefs that make up our worldview live? They are kept in the treasuries of our heart and soul—the deep sanctums of our being. Since most of the basic beliefs about life and reality that we hold were formed when we were children, it should not be surprising that when we seek to storm those treasuries and sanctuaries of the heart, the gatekeeper who blocks the way is the "child" within us. When we speak to the child within with whimsical parables and stories, we often gain access to the basic beliefs and values that might otherwise be denied. It is the Spirit of God that ultimately speaks to the depths of the human heart, but we know from the Spirit's work in the life and ministry of Christ that he often uses stories to penetrate the soul. The commentary section speaks to the "adult" within us, making possible mature understanding and mature decisions based on biblical truth.

In the pages ahead we will meet lordly lions and hassled husbands, Scrooges and Huck Finns, private investigators and perturbed insects. Through their stories, truths about the Bible, the Trinity, creation, providence, Fall and redemption will be explored. It is also hoped that these truths will be taken deep into the minds and lives of those who read them.

How might individuals, groups, or classes best use a book like this? Let me address this question by first making a suggestion or two for every reader. Read the parables slowly. Enjoy them without rushing through. You may find it helpful after finishing the parable to think through the questions on the parable (found at the end of each chapter) before moving on to the commentary. Don't try to work through all the questions— you'll get bogged down—but select a few. After working through some of the questions on the parable (part one of the question section), read through the commentary section that follows.

For small group use, encourage the members of the group to read the parable and think through some of the parable questions in advance of the group discussion. The commentary section may be assigned as optional reading. The leader, however, should be thoroughly familiar with the commentary and be prepared to point out some of the leading ideas or key statements to the group during the discussion of the parable. For classroom use the teacher may want to read the parable aloud (perhaps having students read the dialogue for different characters) and then discuss it using the parable questions. It might then be valuable to reserve the next class meeting for the discussion of the commentary. Students should come having worked through the commentary and questions on their own as well as having read the relevant material in a standard theological textbook. This kind of preparation would make possible a more intensive probing and processing of the doctrine.

So having warned you about what to expect and how you might proceed, I return to Huck and Jim. While I sympathize with Huck, I now feel a lot more like Jim. The longer I'm on the journey, the more I find that good theology (not the trendy stuff but the classic kind, rooted in Scripture and echoed in every generation of the church) comes in very handy. I invite you, therefore, to think hard but have fun. It is my hope and prayer that thinking pilgrims will find in these parables and in the comments that accompany them useful maps that will lead to a deeper enjoyment of God.

Take, for instance, the case of Ralph, one of the characters in our first parable. It is just such an enjoyment of God that he is seeking. But some obstacles seem to block the way. Can theology really help Ralph address his troubles? Let's find out.

Acknowledgments

One bit of housekeeping needs to be done before we proceed. I have the pleasant task of saying thank you to a number of wonderful people. My debts to family and friends are large ones, never to be repaid. But let me make an installment payment by acknowledging the encouragement received from so many. I begin with my colleagues and students at Seminary of the East and Scott Theological College. Paul Sorrentino and Lou Soiles, InterVarsity staff workers and former students of mine, gave special encouragement to a person easily discouraged. Cynthia Bunch-Hotaling, the InterVarsity Press editor with whom I worked most closely on this project, offered one good idea after another. Family in Canada and in the States were always enthusiastic about the project and patient with me and my moods over the years when I was chipping away at the ideas presented in these pages. My children, Anne and Jonathan, were gracious listeners and critics of early versions of many of the parables found in this book. My greatest debt among earthly creditors, however, is to my wife, Lois, for her love, her encouragement, her ideas, and her friendship.

Chapter One
Doing Theology:
The Trouble
with Ralph

The softball game was over and Ralph, Rob, and Sammy walked to the parking lot, pleased with the game and ready to celebrate with coffee at Denny's. The three friends were on the same company team, Silicon Software. Tonight they had smothered Green Valley Chemical 9 to 3. Rob had three hits; Sammy had pitched a six hitter but Ralph had made three errors at shortstop and had played like his glove was made of cement. The three of them enjoyed their friendship a great deal though it was not without some tensions. They were all Christians, elders in their local church and went way back with each other. Their conversations were always stimulating.

An hour later Rob, Ralph, and Sammy were finishing their coffee, chuckling together in their booth. Rob changed the course of the conversation by asking Ralph about Beth. Beth was Ralph's wife of fifteen years and two children. Ten of those years had been great, the last five not so great.

"She's okay," Ralph said reluctantly. "Not much change."

"Is she eating?" Sammy asked.

Eating. It should have been a funny question. But in Beth's case it wasn't. Beth had been diagnosed as anorexic. "No problem," said the doctor. "Anorexia is very treatable nowadays." "No problem," the hospital said during several of Beth's month-long stints on rehab. "No problem," said the long line of psychiatrists and counselors. "No problem," said the pastor and church members and family. But there was a problem, a growing one. Beth was still not eating. She was down to ninety pounds. Ralph's insurance had stopped paying the medical bills. He was thousands in the red and sinking deeper every month. He had been warned at work about his frequent absences.

"No, she's not eating," Ralph said very flatly.

Sammy and Rob knew what that simple answer meant for Ralph physically. It meant all-night vigils, forced feedings, injections, intravenous, desperate prayers. Ralph's errors at shortstop tonight were symptoms of the physical toll Beth's illness was taking.

Rob spoke. "Look, Ralph, I know it's none of my business and you know we both love Beth. But we've watched you now for five years and it's not getting any better." Rob paused, reluctant to continue.

"What I'm trying to say, Ralph, is that . . . don't you think you've given enough? I mean if Beth doesn't want to change . . . after all she's the one that has refused to accept help and has put you through hell. What I'm trying to say is that you've got grounds. Nobody likes to walk away from a marriage, but you're destroying yourself by hanging on. Doesn't God want you to be happy and enjoy him? How can you in your situation?"

Rob lapsed into an uncomfortable silence. He had wanted to say this to Ralph for months. How long do you sit and watch quietly while your buddy comes apart at the seams? He had watched and said nothing while Ralph's face became that of an old man; he had watched his friend's spirit break and his money disappear. Even Christians had to recognize that nothing is more evil than to destroy someone's self-image and esteem. Rob had come to the conclusion that God's love for us meant that we were worthwhile. Beth was destroying the work of God's love in Ralph's life because his sense of being worthwhile was disappearing. For the sake of the gospel, which declares that God died to save us and help us to become all that we could be, Ralph should leave Beth. She was undermining the work of the gospel in his life. How could God be pleased when someone spurned his divine love, became self-destructive and began destroying others around her? Rob's thoughts were broken by Sammy's angry voice.

"Do you hear yourself, Rob? Do you realize what you're suggesting?" Sammy asked. "You know as well as I do what the Bible says about divorce, what our church says about it, and how our mothers and fathers feel about it." Sammy was angry because Rob's comment was so typical. Rob was Mr. "Do-what-makes-you-happy." Sammy saw Rob as a Christian hedonist who bent the gospel to suit his own tastes, to get out from under responsibilities he didn't like. Sammy had seen him do this time and again as an elder. There was no question about his commitment to Christ or the church or his wife, but Sammy still didn't like the sound of Rob's advice.

"You know, Rob," Sammy went on, his temper rising, "I've always appre-

ciated your friendship; and for that reason I've put up with your trendy values
and attitudes, but you've gone too far this time. Obeying God has nothing to do
with our happiness or joy. You do what is right because God says so and that's
it. Divorce is against God's law." Sammy then turned to Ralph.

"Don't listen to this stuff, Ralph. Christian living involves suffering. Forget
this 'joy' business and keep doing the right thing. God will bless you if you obey
his law, but he will curse you if you disobey. Obedience, not happiness, has
been my motivation as a Christian, as an elder, and as a husband. Your job is to
be faithful, not joyful."

Ralph looked into the faces of his two friends. He spoke to Rob first.

"I don't know whether to punch you in the mouth or hug you as a brother."
He stirred the coffee grounds that remained in the bottom of his cup and then
Ralph continued, "Beth needs me. Divorce is not an option. Doesn't the gospel
say something about loving the unlovable, even your enemies? There's something about God and his gospel that tells me that one-way love, even when it
means suffering, is okay. There's something about what the Bible teaches about
creation that tells me to value people—who are all created in God's image—
even when they're scarred and distorted by sin and the Fall. God never gives up
on his creatures and neither should we. There's always something worth
redeeming, something worth loving, something worth hoping for.

"You feel sorry for me because I've been doing all the giving. It's funny,
Rob, and I don't mean to be offensive, but I've often had this longing for you
to know the joy and happiness in God that comes from depending upon him and
desiring him even when you're up to your eyeballs in problems." Ralph took a
sip and then turned to Sammy.

"I hear your concern for me to obey God and not just do the selfish thing.
Yet I hear you call for a joyless obedience that doesn't seem to square with
Scripture or the experience of great saints in the past like Augustine and
Jonathan Edwards who obeyed God primarily out of a relentless desire to enjoy
him. You told me to do the right thing but for the wrong reason. Christian
hedonism is the only thing that has kept me going over the last five years.

"The toughest thing I've had to deal with is not Beth's medical problems but
my natural allergy to God. I've doubted his love and questioned his goodness
and shaken my fist at him with anger. But it's that aversion to God that has been
the source of my greatest misery and deepest despair. It has been my pursuit of
joy in God through Christ that has been the only antidote to this allergy."

Not much more was said that night about marriage and church and duty. The
friends soon left and went to their own homes in silence. They would gather
again next week, maybe talk about these things again and try to figure out just

what the trouble was with Ralph. Maybe things would change. Maybe, each thought, the other would see the light.

The Theology Behind the Story: Doing Theology

What does a postgame conversation over a cup of coffee among three aging softball warriors have to do with learning theology? Quite a bit, actually. That is what I want to point out in this commentary. Believe it or not, theology, at least biblical theology, is concerned with all of life. Remember that great verse in Colossians 3:17: "And whatever you do, whether in word or deed, do it all in the name of the Lord Jesus, giving thanks to God the Father through him"? If I follow Christ as Lord and seek to live the whole of my life under his lordship, then I am looking at all of life from a "theological" perspective.

Ralph was trying to do that in the parable—look at all of life from a theological perspective. He seemed to believe that good theology could help him produce a lifestyle of glad obedience. The trouble is, not every Christian feels that way about theology. I've met some believers who feel so alienated from the discipline that they even pit the Bible against theology as if the two were enemies.

Ralph is heading in a different direction, however. What can his story teach us? I'd like to explore two major ideas drawn from the parable—the importance of theology and the definition of theology.

Why Theology Is Important

You knew theology was important before you met Ralph. Yet you might have harbored some suspicions that it was also dangerous to your faith or too detached from your daily life as a Christian pilgrim. As I think about Ralph's struggle to keep his marriage alive and to keep his faith alive, I see Christian theology acting as a powerful ally fueling both his love for God and his obedience to God's will as a husband. He says at one point after Rob has suggested that Ralph consider divorce that "there's something about what the Bible teaches about creation that tells me to value people, who all are created in God's image, even when they're scarred and distorted by sin and the Fall." Ralph's theological convictions keep him from giving up on Beth. Let me list some benefits of theology that Ralph's story suggests, either directly or by implication: *Theology is important for self-understanding.* In the parable Ralph shows some confusion about who he is as a believer and what he should do. At one point he says to Rob, "I don't know whether to punch you in the mouth or hug you as a brother." Later he confesses that "the toughest thing I've had to deal with is not Beth's medical problems but my natural allergy toward God." Ralph's attempts at self-understanding, at sorting out his own feelings and convictions, leads him to think about his relationship with God. Ralph's attempts at self-understanding lead him to theological reflection. John Calvin, the great sixteenth-century Protestant theologian, was convinced that theological reflection was necessary for self-understanding:

> Nearly all wisdom we possess, that is to say, true and sound wisdom, consists of two parts: the knowledge of God and of ourselves. . . . No one can look upon himself without immediately turning his thoughts to the contemplation of God, in whom he "lives and moves". . . . Again, it is certain that man never achieves a clear knowledge of himself unless he has first looked upon God's face, and then descends from contemplating him to scrutinize himself. For we always seem to ourselves righteous and upright and wise and holy. . . . if we look merely to ourselves and not also to the Lord.[1]

To understand ourselves we need to know God. Theology helps us to gain that double understanding.

Theology is important for our relationship with God and others. Ralph was able to cope in his relationships with God and his wife because of his theological convictions. Our relationship with God and others depends on theological truth. Millard Erickson points to this benefit of theology by quoting Hebrews 11:6: "And without faith it is impossible to please God, because anyone who comes to him must believe that he exists and that he rewards those who earnestly seek him." Erickson observes that the "author does not mean that one who attempts to approach God may be rejected because of lack of such a faith in him, but that one would not even attempt to approach God unless he already had this belief."[2]

Similarly, we can improve our relationship with others by understanding biblical truth. Paul Vitz has documented how modern society pro-

motes a worldview and lifestyle that is so self-absorbed that it makes relationships of depth and commitment virtually impossible. The theological resources of the Christian, by contrast, can deliver him from such a trap: The individual Christian, at least if he is serious, has many guides to keep him away from extreme selfishness. First there is the love of God, expressed in faith and in contemplative and meditative prayer. There is also the Christian's awareness of man's deep potential for sin and the need to be alert to the traps and delusions of the world. . . . There is . . . Christian doctrine, the creeds, the communion of saints. All these combine to help the practicing Christian not only keep from surrendering to the persistent desire to return to selfism but also arrive at higher levels of love and spiritual knowledge.[3]
To improve the quality of our relationships with God and others is both a goal and a benefit of Christian theology.

Theology is also important for society. Our three friends in the restaurant didn't get into politics, but the ideas and values they expressed, if enlarged to society-wide proportions, would have a marked impact. Ideas do make an impact on society. Who could deny the impact on society of Hitler's racial theories, Lenin's political ideas, or Darwin's notion of evolution? Similarly, Christian theology has had its impact. "How many hospitals," writes Millard Erickson, "how many institutions of higher education have come into being because of the driving force of those who went forth in the name of the one they believed to be God Incarnate?"[4] G. K. Chesterton boldly stated that every departure from orthodox theology (such as Arianism, pantheism, scientism) has led to political oppression. "There is only one thing that can never go past a certain point in its alliance with oppression—and that is orthodoxy."[5]

This does not mean that all Christians will have the same political views. It does mean they will share some necessary assumptions that make possible a just society, such as the necessity of law, the value of the individual and of individual rights, etc. Orthodox theology provides the firm spiritual ground that society depends on for its foundation.

Theology is important for worship. Rob described his view of God differently than Sammy or Ralph would. What difference would Rob's theology make Sunday morning at 11:00 a.m.? What are we to think if we are led in a song about the unbreakable moral goodness of humanity, or led in a prayer about how good God is to lead us to himself through many different religions? We would immediately sense that something was wrong with these expressions of corporate worship. But we should not miss the fact that our theological understanding gave us the sense to detect some breach of true worship. Thomas Watson, the seventeenth-century Puritan writer, argued that Christians "should be grounded in the essential points of religion, and have their foundation well laid"; otherwise "we can never worship God acceptably."[6] Though it is often pointed out, we must never forget that the great commandment in Matthew 22:37 includes loving God with our minds. Doing theology is important for true worship.

Theology is important for the integrity of the church. At one point in the parable Sammy in his own mind admits that Rob is committed to the church and is a leader in the church. Yet he feels that Rob has a very selfish view of what the church is all about. Sammy seems worried about the impact of Rob's theological convictions on the church. Wrong theological convictions can begin to affect the church, particularly when leaders fall into error or act pragmatically, not taking the time to find sufficient theological guidance before making decisions. Heresies and rival ideologies beat against the walls of the church and threaten its life.

We don't have to agree with Sammy on everything to recognize that his concern for the purity of the church in the realm of ideas is a valid one. Theology matters when it comes to the health of the church.

Theology is an important aid to interpreting the Bible. The three friends in the story all refer to the Bible directly or indirectly, and yet each interprets it differently. For Sammy the Bible is a law book, and everything is strained through that theological grid. For Rob the Bible is concerned about the happiness of humanity. That becomes a key for Rob in interpreting the Bible. Ralph's key is still something else. In each case theological assumptions shape the way the Bible is interpreted. We might be tempted to conclude that the only way to avoid twisting Scripture is to suspend all our theological conviction when we come to the text of the Bible. This is neither possible nor desirable. I agree with Thomas Watson that orthodox theology

is the golden key that opens the chief mysteries of religion; it gives us a whole system and body of divinity, exactly drawn in all its linea-

ments and lively colors; it helps us to understand many of those difficult things which occur in the reading of the word; it helps to untie many Scripture knots.[7]
In summary, the above benefits of theological study correct the notion that theology is just for ivory towers and classroom bull sessions. Truth is for life. These benefits should give us great incentive to pursue the serious work of doing theology. But before we can do theology, shouldn't we define what it is? Ralph can help us here as well.

Theology Defined: The Art and Science of Enjoying God

The parable not only speaks of the importance of theology; it also says something about the nature of theology. Something Ralph said got me thinking about the definition of theology. Ralph was making a confession about what was the hardest challenge he had to face:

> The toughest thing I've had to deal with is not Beth's medical problems but my natural allergy to God. I've doubted his love and questioned his goodness and shaken my fist at him with anger. But it's that aversion to God that has been the source of my greatest misery and deepest despair. It has been my pursuit of joy in God through Christ that has been the only antidote to this allergy.

Ralph's confession tells me that true theology should be problem-solving, not just information-gathering. What I mean by this is that we should define theology in terms of what it should do, what problem it seeks to solve. Take the example of defining a hospital. I could define it abstractly as a place with doctors and machines and nurses and beds full of patients. That would be a descriptive definition. A more useful definition would be that hospitals are institutions that seek to bring sick or injured people to health. That defines hospital in terms of the problem that needs to be solved—sick or injured people need to become well or healthy.

In the same way we need to define theology functionally. What is the problem that needs solving? Ralph talks about an allergy to God. He speaks about an aversion to God. Both believers and unbelievers wrestle with their feelings of alienation from God. Theology should seek to overcome these feelings of alienation by leading the inquirer into fellowship with and enjoyment of God. Thus, I'd like to propose that *theology is the science and art of enjoying God through Christ in all of life.* Look closer with me at the five parts of this definition.

First, Christian theology is a science concerned with knowing the truth about God and his world. To enjoy God we must know the truth about him and his will. Lies or half-truths will not wash. Since God has spoken in his word, the Bible, we can get fully reliable information about his will and his ways. This is the scientific task of theology where we examine the text and context of Scripture and deduce truths about God in Christ. Theology is a science, for it uses the tool of reason to gather and organize the truths taught in the Bible. Biblical truth becomes the necessary foundation for truth in every other science. Truth in any field becomes the fuel of praise and joy in God.

Second, Christian theology is an art concerned with applying the truth. Ralph reminds us that knowing the truth is not enough. His concern in his relationship with Beth was applying the truth to his marriage. Theology is a science; but it is not only a science, it is also an art. William Perkins, a Cambridge theologian in the age of Shakespeare, wrote that "theology is the science of living blessedly forever."[8] Perkins calls it a science (*scientia*), but it leads to the art of being happy in God ("living blessedly forever").

Theology in this sense is wisdom or *sapientia*, the term Augustine, the brilliant African theologian of the fourth century, preferred. It is concerned with glad obedience to God, holiness before God and, supremely, the experience of delighting in God. Theology must be more than orthodoxy (right belief). Theology involves orthopraxis (right behavior). Theology thus seeks to change the face of reality by bringing our worshipful service of God into all areas of life. But it is still more than that.

Third, Christian theology is concerned with enjoying God. This is a strong emphasis in the parable. Ralph tells Rob, "I've often had this longing for you to know the joy and happiness in God that comes from depending upon him and desiring him even when you're up to your eyeballs in problems." Ralph makes the further statement, "I hear your call for a joyless obedience that doesn't seem to square with Scripture or the experience of great saints in the past like Augustine and Jonathan Edwards who obeyed God primarily out of a relentless desire to enjoy him." What is all of this about enjoying God and how does it fit into the task of theology?

Let me agree with Ralph. The great end of theological reflection and wise application is glorifying God by delighting in him. The famous answer to the first question of the Westminster Shorter Catechism reminds us that the "chief end of man is to glorify God and enjoy him forever."

John Piper has argued persuasively that our spiritual ancestors could have improved upon this statement by changing the word "and" to the word "by." Thus the chief purpose of humanity, for Piper, is "glorifying God *by* enjoying him." Because of his emphasis on enjoying God he has labeled his position "Christian hedonism." I find the term a little disturbing, conjuring up images of martini-drinking churchgoers gathering in the church foyer to discuss their latest Caribbean cruise. What does he mean by this term?

Let me quote Piper as he clarifies what he does not mean by the term:
First, Christian hedonism as I use the term does not mean God becomes a means to help us get worldly pleasures. The pleasure Christian hedonism seeks is the pleasure which is in God himself. He is the end of our search, not the means to some further end. Our exceeding joy is he, the Lord—not the streets of gold, or the reunion with relatives or any blessing of heaven. Christian hedonism does not reduce God to a key that unlocks a treasure chest of gold and silver. Rather it seeks to transform the heart so that "the Almighty will be your gold and choice silver to you" (Job 22:25).[9]
Christian hedonism focuses on one pleasure in particular, not any pleasure in general. That one pleasure that is the driving force behind the life and theology and work of the Christian hedonist is delighting in the Lord. Piper clarifies two more misunderstandings:
Second, Christian Hedonism does not make a god out of pleasure. It says that one has already made a god out of whatever he finds most pleasure in. The goal of Christian hedonism is to find most pleasure in the one and only God and thus avoid the sin of covetousness, that is, idolatry (Colossians 3:5). Finally, Christian Hedonism does not put us above God when we seek him out of self-interest. A patient is not greater than his physician.[10]

This last point about seeking God out of self-interest is a sticky one. I believe that being selfish is wrong. But Christian hedonism tells me that I am to seek my own highest interest by seeking to enjoy God. How can we deal with this tension?

Consider Psalm 37:4: "Delight yourself in the LORD and he will give you the desires of your heart." Why is God pleased when I satisfy my need to experience delight by aiming all my desire at him? The reason is simple. God's greatest desire is to be praised—for his worth and beauty to be recognized. This is the necessary foundation of all true worship. "You are worthy, our Lord and God, to receive honor and glory and power" (Rev 4:11). But how is he best praised? When he is shown to be life's highest pleasure and greatest treasure. Without delight in him we give no glory to him.

The Puritans discovered this truth centuries earlier. We sometimes think of Puritans as Christians who had lost all their capacity to have fun, but in fact they were "God-enjoyers" of a very high order. I offer Thomas Watson as proof. His classic theology text, *A Body of Divinity,* tells us, "We glorify God when we are God-admirers; admire his attributes, which are the glistening beams by which the divine nature shines forth; his promises which are the charter of free grace, and the spiritual cabinet where the pearl of price is hid; the noble effects of his power and wisdom in making the world." Watson concludes, "To glorify God is to have God-admiring thoughts; to esteem him most excellent, and search for diamonds in this rock only."[11]

If our chief end is to glorify God by enjoying him, then the task of theology is not exempt from service to the cause of Christian hedonism. True theology must seek to cultivate delight in God and be an expression of that delight. Thomas Aquinas was right: "Theology is taught by God, teaches of God, and leads to God."[12]

Fourth, Christian theology focuses on enjoying God through the Christ of the Scriptures. I desire to fuel my delight in God by engaging in the science and art of theology. But I hit an immediate snag even as I begin. I stumble over the mystery of God's infinite being, the problem of evil and a God who is good, the judgment and wrath of God, my own pride, etc. A thousand obstacles block my path as I begin to do theology to increase my joy in God. What do I do? Where do I begin?

For an evangelical, theology begins not with creation but with the cross, not with speculation on God's invisible glories but on the God who has revealed himself in his "weakness" and the "foolishness" of the cross (1 Cor 1:25). If I try to approach God directly from his works or by reflecting on his infinite attributes, I become a "theologian of glory" (in Martin Luther's famous expression), who is only full of pride in my own reasoning and not able to know God, for my eyes will be blinded by his majesty.

In sharp contrast, true theology is a theology of the cross. Luther reminds us why:

> For because men put to wrong use their knowledge of God which they had gained from his works, God determined on the contrary to be known from sufferings . . . so that from now on it could never be enough for a man, nor could it benefit him to know God in his glory and majesty unless he knows him at the same time in the humility and shame of the cross. In this way he "destroys the wisdom of the wise and brings to nought the understanding of the prudent."[13]

Luther's warning needs to be heard. If we seek to enjoy God by doing theology, we could end full of spiritual pride and spiritual blindness, because we tend, as sinners, to "put to wrong use" our knowledge of God. Only when we look at theology through the perspective of the cross do we have some protection against this danger of a theology of glory.

We must not trust reason or experience alone to know God and enjoy him. God will be a puzzle and problem to us if we seek to know him from circumstances. God is revealed best where he is hidden most—in the dark shadows of weakness and defeat that surround his death on the cross. Our joy in him increases with our vision of him as redeemer, for we can see his heart revealed on the cross—God who is for us and not against us. Such a God is a delight and not a terror.

Fifth, Christian theology seeks to equip the believer to enjoy God in all of life. Instead of leading to the enjoyment of God, theology can go bad and lead us away from God and into the arms of idols—false objects of worship or security. What are some of the ways theology can go bad? The parable points to a couple. Rob is steering close to something that we would call selfism. I'll try to explain that later when we discuss the authority of the Bible. Sammy is falling into other ditches. One might be dead orthodoxy—a kind of loveless adherence to theology that smacks of legalism and pride. Theology goes bad when it does not lead to the enjoyment of the triune God of the Bible but leads to glorying in and desiring something or someone else more than the biblical God. Sammy and Rob represent just a few of the pitfalls that a young theologian (or an old one for that matter) can fall into.

One of the most common pitfalls for evangelical theology is that of *dualism*. Dualism sets the higher things (the spiritual, intellectual, or religious) above the lower things (material, sensual or secular) and makes the distinction important in many of its theological formulations. Dualism teaches that the Bible (and theology) is concerned about higher things such as our soul, salvation and God's glory but is relatively unconcerned about lower things of daily life such as business, sports, or economics. No one admits to being a dualist. It is more a subtle way of thinking than it is a conscious intellectual choice. The danger comes when the Bible and theology no longer speak to a worldview but are restricted to the areas of religion or personal piety.

A *worldview* is a comprehensive way of thinking about everything. The South Sea islander sees the same sun that the Manhattan stockbroker sees, but the two interpret it differently because they have a different set of basic values and beliefs. The South Sea islander sees it as a sign of his god's favor. The stockbroker sees it as a time marker reminding him that he has only two hours to close the deal.

If my theology does not become part of a comprehensive biblical worldview—God's view of things—then several problems occur.

First of all, my enjoyment of God will be seriously restricted, for I cannot pursue my enjoyment of him in all of life. I can seek to delight in him when I read my Bible and pray and witness or worship. But dualism teaches that God is not really interested in the softball game or the business luncheon or the art exhibit or the new technology at work. My involvement in the game, the luncheon, the exhibit or the technology becomes peripheral to glorifying God and enjoying him. I become alienated from him in my work or leisure.

Second, I might be captured by a competing ideology that is at odds with Christian truth. Albert Wolters warns of this danger:

> The scope of biblical teaching includes such ordinary "secular" matters as labor, social groups, and education. Unless such matters are

approached in terms of a worldview based squarely on such central scriptural categories as creation, sin, and redemption, our assessment of these supposedly nonreligious dimensions of our lives will likely be dominated by a competing worldview of the secularized west.[14] Third, I might fall into an unwitting idolatry. If I accept dualism I will be blinded to the real spiritual danger that lurks in all the "peripheral" areas. If my theology does not enable me to look at, say, our national defense policy and critique its theological implications from a Christian basis, then how do I keep from falling into an idolatrous dependence on missiles and star wars for my security instead of finding my security in the true and living God? Major areas of life become "autonomous" or independent from my discipleship. My heart can begin to treasure the autonomous security, satisfaction or pleasure found in the exhibit or the new computer or the political party, and God is pushed to the sidelines.

We will be returning to this issue of dualism throughout this study and particularly when we discuss the doctrine of creation. For now we simply point out the danger of any split-level thinking and affirm that theology is the science and art of enjoying God through Christ *in all of life*. I would further affirm that the doctrines we will be looking at in the upcoming chapters—the authority of the Bible, the Trinity and majesty of God, the goodness of creation and providence, the reality of sin and the truth of redemption—are all powerful forces in overcoming dualism and unleashing the enjoyment of God. At least Ralph found them to be so.

Let me be more specific and state the five central convictions that give me hope and help in my quest to overcome dualism and glorify God by enjoying him.

The first conviction concerns the ultimate authority of the Bible. How can I know the truth? I am headed in the right direction when I affirm in heart and in mind that the triune God has spoken, generally through creation and history, but in a special way through Christ in the Scriptures. The Scriptures, therefore, are the written Word of God and are the error-free source of ultimate truth in all areas of life and reality (this is discussed further in chapter two).

The second conviction concerns the majesty and Trinity of God. What is the heart of reality? I am headed in the right direction when I affirm that the triune God is the heart of reality. From the mutual self-giving and joy that each member of the Trinity finds in the other comes the God-centered love that is behind the creation of all things, the judgment of all things and the redemption of all things (this is discussed further in chapters three and four). The third conviction concerns the goodness of every aspect of creation. Why am I here? I am headed in the right direction when I affirm in heart and mind that the triune God has created all things, including history and culture as well as the natural world, and that they are good because God has made them. Humanity was created in God's image as male and female in order to love him and build God-centered cultures. Central to this task is the institution of marriage and the family (this is discussed further in chapters five and six).

The fourth conviction concerns the cosmic scope of the Fall and sin. What's wrong with me and my world? I am headed in the right direction when I affirm in heart and mind that the human creature has rebelled against the triune God's purpose for human life (God-centered culture building) and that this rebellion is cosmic in scope, extending to humanity's being, society and culture, history and religion. The primary expression of this rebellion is idolatry. Because of this rebellion and idolatry, suffering, evil, and death have been unleashed into human experience. The goodness of creation and culture has been horribly misdirected, being used now for idols rather than for God (this is discussed further in chapter seven).

The fifth conviction concerns the fullness of redemption in Christ. What's the solution to life's problems and the curse that hangs over life? I am headed in the right direction when I affirm in heart and mind that the triune God has not given up on creation, history, and culture, but has chosen to restore and perfect his good but fallen world, transforming it into the kingdom of God where righteousness and peace will dwell. The kingdom of God (the restoration of all things through the lordship of Christ) is established through the Redeemer, Jesus Christ, who, through his death and resurrection and the renewing work of the Holy Spirit, creates a new people of God, the church, as witnesses to the kingdom (this is discussed further in chapter eight).

These affirmations make up a truly evangelical worldview and would lead us, I believe, into a great delight in God. The parables and commentaries that follow will take each key conviction and explore its meaning for the building of a biblical worldview and the cultivating of Christian hedonism.

Conclusion

We've thought quite a bit about Ralph's story. We've looked at two key ideas that the parable seems to teach us about theology, namely that theology is important and that theology is (or should be) the art and science of enjoying God through Christ in all of life.

Ralph's trouble is really a challenge we all face—how to have a living faith that pursues its joy in God even in the midst of hardships. My strong conviction is that good theology based on the truths of God's word regarding creation, Fall, and redemption can help us build a faith that works. Such a faith can lead us to the satisfaction of glorifying God by delighting him.

Questions for Individuals or for Group Discussion

Part One

1. How would you define "doing theology"?

In what senses are Sammy, Rob and Ralph "doing theology" in this parable?

2. Ralph refers to Christian hedonism as a summary of his theological convictions. What does he seem to mean by this term in the context?

3. Do Rob's criticisms discredit the idea of Christian hedonism? Explain.

How would Rob define that term?

How would Sammy define it?

4. How would you distinguish Ralph's position on Christian hedonism from the other two?

What are the strengths and weaknesses of his position?

5. How would you explain what Ralph meant when he said that it was not Beth's sickness but his "aversion to God that has been the source of my greatest misery and deepest despair"?

How have you seen this to be true in general for believers?

6. Ralph went on to say: "It has been my pursuit of joy in God through

Christ that has been the only antidote to this allergy." What themes in Scripture seem to support this idea?

What themes challenge it?

7. What roles do the doctrines of God, the Bible, humanity, sin and redemption play in this parable?

What has made them more than merely abstractions for the characters in the parable, particularly Ralph?

Part Two

8. Of the benefits of theology mentioned in the "Theology Behind the Story" section, which ones appeal most to you? Why?

9. Is it true to say that theology is an art? a science? Do you prefer one concept over the other, or neither? Explain.

10. Evaluate Piper's argument that Christian hedonism is the proper way to glorify God. What are the dangers in this approach? What are the benefits?

11. What does dualism look like in practice?

How can the doctrines of creation, fall and redemption help overcome dualism?

12. Review the list of five key convictions for a Christian worldview. Which ones raise the most questions in your mind?

Which ones make the most sense to you?

For Further Reading

For a basic and highly readable overview of Christian doctrine I recommend Bruce Milne's *Know the Truth* (Downers Grove, Ill.: InterVarsity Press, 1982). For more information on the theme of glorifying God by enjoying him, see John Piper's *Desiring God: Meditations of a Christian Hedonist* (Portland: Multnomah Press, 1986). Albert Wolters's *Creation Regained: Biblical Basics for a Reformational Worldview* (Grand Rapids: Eerdmans, 1985) is a brief but stimulating introduction to the discussion of worldviews in general and the Reformational worldview in particular. For a more involved and scholarly discussion of narrative theology, see the useful collection of key articles and excerpts in Stanley Hauerwas and L. Gregory Jones, eds., *Why Narrative? Readings in Narrative Theology* (Grand Rapids: Eerdmans, 1989).

Chapter Two
Scripture:
The Gift of Arthur

T*here was no doubt about it.* King Arthur was dead. If someone wanted evidence of the fact, all they had to do was look at Sir Galahad curled up by the window in a fetal position. His blank face was as white as the pale snow drifting outside the cottage walls. Ever since the death of Arthur by the hand of Mordred at the battle of Camlan, Galahad had been beyond comfort. Since that tragedy some months ago, the youthful Galahad—a mere nineteen-year-old—had aged like new fruit stung by an untimely frost. Those who loved this youth feared for his life.

High on the list of those who loved him most was Gildas, now standing in front of the fire stirring a stew for lunch. This aged and overweight squire of the young Galahad was a complete contrast to his master, the slender adolescent who only three years earlier had been accepted by Arthur as a knight of the Round Table. But Gildas differed from Galahad in more than weight and age. Many a horse had bolted from seeing Gildas approach, convinced their backs would be broken by this barrel of a man, nearly as round as he was tall. I wish I could say that Gildas was as swift of mind as he was round of shape, but that would not be true. He was a man of few thoughts and many pounds.

Yet Gildas, the light of the fire glowing in his plump face, was stirring more than stew this dark late winter's day. He was at his wit's end as to what to do about his master. Here it was, the Thursday before Easter, and Galahad seemed unmoved by the pending celebration of our Lord's resurrection. Gildas could not take another day of deathlike silence and another night hearing Galahad scream in his sleep wild things about "broken promises." He needed a bold idea.

He needed something that could shake his master from this terrible depression. Just as he was slapping a boiled chunk of turnip with his spoon, an idea came to him. An idea—a bold one at that—had come bubbling up in the simple kettle of his small brain. Gildas was hatching a plan to save his master's life. He would journey to Avalon, the island where Arthur's body was rumored to be buried. There he would find the tomb. He would enter the tomb and take from it some relic from Arthur's belongings—his coat of mail, or the small dagger he had used. Gildas would bring the relic back and give it to Galahad. Then the squire would watch while the relic did its magic by restoring Galahad's will to live.

He planned to leave before dawn on the next day—Good Friday—while his master slept. He could not help but chuckle to himself. Imagine him, Gildas the Rotund, embarking on a great quest! Yet silly or not, he resolved to find his way to Avalon and back, or die in the attempt.

The sun was still sleeping and the snow still falling as Gildas, mounted on his long-suffering steed, Samson, began his journey to Avalon. He rode day and night, Friday and Saturday, stopping only to cook soup for warmth and strength. He saw no dragons. He fought no battles except with fatigue and despair. Just after midnight Saturday, the faint aroma of saltwater and ocean strand teased his senses. By sunrise on Sunday morning he stood at Land's End, wind and spray slapping his unwashed face. Gazing out into the fog of the Atlantic, Gildas could make out the faint outline of Avalon. But how was he to get there?

Gildas looked far down the shore to see whether any fishermen were planning to break the fourth commandment by fishing on the Lord's day. For the right price he hoped he might hire one to take him to the island. He spotted a figure standing by a boat with a single sail several hundred yards away. As Gildas walked toward the figure he saw that the man was cloaked in a black monk's cowl; the hood of the cowl was gathered closely about the man's face, obscuring all detail.

"Blessed Easter morning to you, friend," Gildas said as cheerfully as he could. The hooded figure bowed slightly but said nothing. Gildas decided to continue. "What would be the chances of hiring this boat for a little Easter excursion out to the island of Avalon?"

The man said nothing but slowly swept an arm toward the boat and stood as if frozen in that pose. Gildas was frightened, but for the sake of his master climbed into the boat. The figure in black pushed the boat from shore. Soon they were tacking through the strong winds and high waves toward Avalon.

Several hours later, Gildas stood on the cold sand of Avalon's beach. His companion pulled the boat further onto shore and began walking up through the dunes toward a marble structure that Gildas assumed must be the tomb of Arthur. The figure stopped in front of the tomb and pointed to the inscription above the entrance which read: "Here lies Arthur, High King of Britain." Gildas felt tears on his soiled cheeks as he thought of the hope that had died in his own heart with the death of his sovereign. But he remembered his purpose. He must break into the tomb now and seize some relic for his master. Gildas's hand rested on the handle of the dagger dangling from his belt. If the dark figure tried to stop him, thought Gildas, he must stop his blade first.

Gildas pushed on the door of the tomb. To his surprise the door gave way easily. The hooded figure stood motionless. Gildas entered the tomb and, in the light of the early morning sun streaming through the door, began to scan the interior. Various pieces of armor were strewn around. In the center was the great stone coffin. The lid was lying broken in two on the floor. Gildas walked slowly toward the open casket. What would the lifeless face look like? What ravages had death inflicted on the king's countenance over these last months?

To his shock Gildas saw only an empty coffin. He heard a laugh behind him and turned to face the man standing in the tomb entrance, his figure rimmed in light. The hood was thrown back. It was Arthur! He was alive. As he spoke, Gildas fell to his knees and nearly fainted from an overwhelming mixture of fear, joy, and sleepless nights. But he fought to stay conscious.

"You have done well to come here, brave Gildas. You seek some magic to save your young master's life. You will find no magic here, however, only the power of the Most High God. I will send you back with a gift to restore the joy of Galahad and all who love my name and have grieved at my death."

"Can't you come back with me yourself and show yourself to Galahad?" asked Gildas.

"It is not yet time for me to return to Britain. One day in its hour of greatest need I shall return, but that hour has not yet come."

Then Arthur reached under his cowl, pulled out a book and handed it to Gildas, who took it with an unsteady hand. The scent of the oiled leather and the gleam of its gilded edges seemed to chase the smell and specter of death from the tomb. Gildas looked at the book's title. He was not good with letters but could make out most of what it said: *The book of Arthur, High King of Britain, written for the joy of all his noble subjects by Uther and Yrgenus, the Royal Parents of the King, and with the faithful cooperation of Merlin, servant of Arthur and sage of England.* Gildas thumbed through the pages with mounting excitement.

It was like a scrapbook containing bits and pieces about Arthur: genealogies of aunts and uncles, high points of his life, diary entries, trips, battles and expeditions. It was indeed a book about Arthur all the way through. Near the end were stories about Arthur and Galahad and all the other knights of the Round Table. The beginnings of Camelot, the coming of Arthur, his many adventures with his friends, how he had to go away but would return one day—all these were contained in this wonderful book. Gildas was surprised to see these stories written, for he had known some of these events as his own personal experiences. The very last chapter of the book told not only about Arthur's death at Camlan but how the High God had brought Arthur back to life on Avalon and how the king would return one day to restore England to its glory. The book was good at producing delight in knowing and loving Arthur, for Gildas was feeling those very emotions now as he read.

The king spoke. Gildas looked up. "Take this book back to Galahad. It will restore him. Tell him to spread its message and send copies of it throughout the kingdom so that it might bring restoration to those who are in despair. Tell them that when the book is embraced, my presence will be experienced and my power unleashed."

Then suddenly, like the darting of a trout, Arthur was gone. Gildas ran to the doorway of the tomb and looked in every direction. There was no trace of him anywhere.

Gildas looked down at the book, tucked it under his arm and made his way back to the mainland in the boat. Samson was waiting patiently just where he had been left. Gildas climbed onto his steed and began the journey back to Camelot full of wonder and excitement.

After three days Gildas was in sight of the towers of Camelot. The snow had melted everywhere, and crocuses and daffodils were popping through the earth. Within an hour he would give the book to Galahad and would be able to watch his grief lift and his joy return.

Riders were coming toward him on the main road. As they came nearer he recognized them as Sir Gawain the Celt, Father Geoffrey of the cathedral, and Sister Charis, headmistress of the Camelot academy. Gildas regarded each of these three as friends of Galahad and beckoned them to stop. They pulled up beside him and listened as he told them of the great quest he had been on and of the priceless book he had been given.

After listening to Gildas go on a bit too long about empty tombs and resurrected bodies and books of wonder, Sir Gawain grabbed the book out of Gildas's hands. Gildas told Sir Gawain to read the last part about why the stories had been written and how Arthur was the key to the whole story of Camelot.

Sir Gawain read for a few minutes, and then looking up he said sternly, "I don't like it. Nothing at all about Celts here. Only hero is Arthur. How about the time I dragged him out of the river when he was a wee lad? Hardly gets a mention. I don't like it, and furthermore, I don't think you got this from Arthur or that he's walking around alive as you claim."

Gildas was flabbergasted by Sir Gawain's words and insisted that Arthur had given him the book personally but that he'd gone away, so they couldn't go to him to prove it.

"Then until you get King Arthur over to my chambers in person, I can only regard the scrapbook as an irrelevant collection of useless, and probably false, information. Scrapbooks never did count for much with me anyway." Sir Gawain passed the book to Father Geoffrey and then spurred his horse and trotted off down the road.

"I must concur with my learned friend," said Father Geoffrey. "I heard nothing about the importance of the clergy in the scrapbook's account of the history of Camelot. While I have the greatest admiration for the late king, I would hardly give him the prominence in the city's life that quite properly should go to the members of my religious order. Ever since I was a seminary student, I was told of the coming of our order to Camelot, how they drove away the druids and made it safe for others to come and live. I follow the wisdom of the ancients, not the musings of a scrapbook. And anything Merlin had a hand in can hardly be trusted." After delivering this little speech, the good father handed the book to the headmistress and continued on his way.

Poor Gildas was sinking lower and lower into his saddle when Sister Charis spoke: "As a teacher of medieval literature, I do believe that the scrapbook is probably genuine. I think the late King Arthur is the most important person in all the history of Camelot. I don't think I am. I would need to look through this scrapbook more carefully though, because I suspect that it is probably filled with bunk, even if the main accounts are right. When I get around to it, I'll give it a look. Greetings to Galahad." And with that she sped off after her departed companions.

Gildas tried to remember what had happened back at the island, tried to get the words just spoken on the road out of his head as he made his way home, but his mind was wrapped in fog, and only the words of the book's critics could be remembered.

He opened the door to the stable, got Samson settled in his stall with water and hay, and then sat on a stool in the corner. He lit a candle that was standing on a table beside him. Then he laid the book on the table. He looked at the book long and hard. He wasn't sure he wanted to give it to Galahad after all. When leaders like Sir Gawain and Father Geoffrey had dismissed it as false, what right did a dolt like himself have to insist that it was true? Even the gracious Sister

Charis felt it was "full of bunk," though she liked the parts about Arthur. His trip was a failure. But it was no use sitting and feeling sorry for oneself. Might as well go in and face the music like a man. If Galahad wanted to dismiss him for his reckless and misguided quest, then so be it.

When Gildas entered the cottage with the controversial book under his arm, he found Galahad sitting at the window just as he had left him. Gildas coughed. Galahad turned slowly and looked at his squire. Gildas was at a loss for words. He simply held up the book and hung his head down.

Galahad uncurled himself. He walked to Gildas and took the book from him very slowly. Galahad read the title of the book and his eyes narrowed. He took the book back to the window and began to thumb through its pages. "Mind the last chapter, Sire," said Gildas with a shiver in his voice.

Galahad read the last chapter and all the chapters before it. The cathedral bell chimed midnight just as Galahad finished the book of Arthur. "This is it, Gildas," Galahad said—the first words he had uttered in months.

"Beg your pardon, Sire?" Gildas responded, not sure that he knew what "it" was.

"This is the gift that Arthur promised me just before he died. He told me not to worry that he would be going away for a while, but that he would give me a gift that would keep his memory alive and make his presence felt. After his death and the wait of many weeks I gave up on his dying promise. But this is it! Gildas, I feel Arthur's presence here in this cottage when I read this book. I believe that what he stood for will not die with him, but that his ideals will continue and triumph in Britain and that he shall return just as promised."

This was too much for Gildas. Wiping his eyes with one hand and grabbing his cutting board and knife with the other, he pretended to be busy in the kitchen, dropping his cuttings and spilling meal everywhere. "What was that, Sire? Just straightening up the kitchen some."

But he knew exactly what Galahad had said; knew that all would be restored; knew that the book his master held in his hands was not just a gift *from* Arthur; knew that for those who embraced it with joy it could become the gift *of* Arthur—a book that communicated his presence and power. And that, thought Gildas to himself, was a bold idea indeed.

The Theology Behind the Story: The Doctrine of Scripture

Gildas's adventure is full of surprises. He is surprised when Arthur gave him the scrapbook. He is surprised by the joy that the book gave to him and his master. He is also surprised by the negative reactions of Sir Gawain, Father Geoffrey and Sister Charis.

My own experience of the Bible reminds me of the experience of Gildas. The Bible has been a book of life and power for me. Yet sometimes the objections of the Bible's critics have cooled my own zeal for the Word. Perhaps you feel this tug in your own heart and mind between love for the Word of God on the one hand and the pull of critics with rival views of truth and authority on the other. Some like Sir Gawain seem to elevate reason above the Bible and look skeptically at its claims to be a unique and supernatural revelation from God. Others like Father Geoffrey seem to object to the Bible because of their own attachment to tradition. When a cherished tradition collides with biblical truth, the Father Geoffrey types will politely side with tradition. Sister Charis has other problems with the book. She reminds me of those who have accepted some of the critical theories of the Bible. They accept some parts as true (and maybe even regard such parts as the Word of God) while rejecting other parts as unreliable.

Galahad, at the end of the story, encounters the book as every disciple of Christ longs to encounter the Bible—as the life-giving Word of God that enables one to grow strong in the enjoyment of God. How do we get to that point? The first conviction among the five listed in the previous chapter points the way to that transforming encounter with the Word:

How can I know the truth? I am heading in the right direction when I affirm in heart and in mind that the triune God has spoken, generally through creation and history, but in a special way through Christ in the Scriptures. The Scriptures, therefore, are the written Word of God and are the source of ultimate truth in all areas of life and reality.

This conviction is echoed in the parable in a number of ways. I would like to look at three ideas from the story that could help deepen our understanding of the doctrine of the Bible. Maybe as these ideas are explored we will agree with Galahad's verdict "This is it!"—not just a gift *from* Christ but a gift *of* Christ, a book that communicates his presence and power.

The Bible as Revelation from God

Gildas is told in the story that the full truth about Arthur can only be known through the Book of Arthur. The last chapter particularly "told not only about Arthur's death at Camlan but how the High God had brought Arthur back to life on Avalon and how the king would return one day to restore England to its glory." In like fashion the Bible affirms to us that those who would know God and find in him their joy must first hear him speak. I'd like to make a few observations about God's revelation of himself to us. Let me mention that I believe God's revelation is necessary, universal and biblical.

First, I note that *God's revelation of himself is necessary*. Revelation can be defined as the "significant self-disclosure of God to man."[1] When I say that revelation is necessary I'm not saying that God had to reveal himself to us. Because God is absolutely free, he didn't have to talk with us at all. He could have kept his presence and identity a secret if he wanted to. But God chose to know us and therefore to talk with us. God wanted to enlist his creatures in the joy and delight of knowing him. This is so basic to the Christian worldview that it is possible to gloss right over it.

But suppose God decided to play "hard to get"? Couldn't we still figure out who he was and what he was like in some way other than revelation? Not really.

Consider these two reasons revelation is necessary if we are to know God. First, we are creatures ("So God created man in his own image," Gen 1:27). While God has made me in his image and likeness, there is still a huge gap between who God is and who I am. This can be called the Creator-creature distinction. This means that God is so vastly different from his creatures in degree as well as in kind that he is incomprehensible. As Bruce Milne observes: "Only God truly knows God." Any thoughts that I might have about God apart from his self-disclosure are pure fictions created in my own imagination and undoubtedly distorted.

Moreover, humankind needs revelation if we are to know God, because we are not only creatures, we are sinners. Milne writes that "our need of revelation is immeasurably increased by our sinfulness." This is because "the fall has affected every aspect of our being, not least our perception of moral and spiritual reality." The sad fact that I must face is that "sin renders us spiritually blind and ignorant of God (Rom 1:18; 1 Cor 1:21; 2 Cor 4:4; Eph 2:1ff.)."[2]

Our need for revelation, if we are to know God and find in him our treasure and pleasure, is absolute. We are helpless to know God unless he takes the initiative. But Christianity is based on the great and glad fact that God has done precisely that—he has shown us who he is and how we can know him. We therefore talk about two distinct kinds of self-disclosure that God has initiated—general and special.

Second, I note that *God's revelation of himself is general and creational.* Before Arthur was known through his book, he was known through his deeds. In the same way we know God first (though often subconsciously) by his works around us and in us. As Psalm 19:1 proclaims: "The heavens declare the glory of God; the skies proclaim the work of his hands."

Romans 1:19-20 builds on Psalm 19 by making clearer that not only does all humanity have some knowledge of the true God and his law, but they will all be judged for how they have responded to the God revealed in creation and history. Paul says bluntly:

What may be known about God is plain to them, because God has made it plain to them. For since the creation of the world God's invisible qualities—his eternal power and divine nature—have been clearly seen, being understood from what has been made, so that men are without excuse.

I hear Paul saying two important things about general revelation in Romans 1:19-20. One is the cosmic scope of general revelation (supporting Psalm 19). God's power and divine nature have been "clearly seen" in creation. I take this to mean that continuously since creation and universally around the earth humankind has known God, that is, they have known their own absolute dependence for life and breath and perception and everything on a power outside themselves. No one makes himself, and no one can sustain her own life for one moment without the sustenance of air and food and water and a thousand other things.

The other point I hear Paul making in Romans 1:19-20 is the "covenantal" character of general revelation. By covenantal I mean that general revelation confronts us with God as *our* king and sovereign, not just as *a* king and sovereign. It is knowledge that obligates us to submit, that demands an appropriate response. This accounts for the universality of religion. God has revealed himself through a "law" that is woven through creation—the law of nature. Because he creates and sustains everything and we are totally dependent on him, we owe him total obedience and worship. What is the actual content of the law of nature? The sense of God within and around your life compels you to "love the Lord your God with all your heart . . . and with all your mind and with all your strength" (Mk 12:30).

What kind of response should we make to the God who shows himself in creation and conscience? The sense of absolute dependence on an all-powerful God should lead to a life of absolute gratitude and total submission. Only such a complete response is worthy of such a complete provision. Have we given God such a total and unqualified response? No. Are there not expressions of religious worship in a thousand cultures around the world? Yes, but in each case the gratitude is limited and the response partial, not absolute and total. Thus Paul must conclude in Romans 3:23, "For all have sinned and fall short of the glory of God": that is, we fall short in loving him with all of our heart, mind, soul and strength.

What are we to do then if general revelation is now misused by our fallen hearts? How can there be true knowledge of God if the subtle but forceful light of nature has been darkened? It is precisely for this reason that the written Word of God was given.

Third, I note that *God's revelation of himself is special and biblical.* The parable centers on the Book of Arthur. In that book the royal family tells the subjects of the realm things that could not otherwise be known about Arthur and his return. In addition the book shows how to enter into renewed fellowship with Arthur after the events of Camlan and Avalon. So it is with the Bible. Jesus Christ is the heart of special revelation from God (Heb 1:2-3). He embodies the self-disclosure of God's wisdom and power in ways more pointed than creation. He also embodies the law of love in a way unequaled in history, thus exposing the sham of rival religions with their compromised demands. His life and death make clear to us that we cannot save ourselves and need to fall upon God's mercy and grace in Christ. All of these specially revealed truths about God and his will are authoritatively recorded for us in God's "scrapbook" about Christ—the Bible. We now turn to take a closer look at this written revelation from God.

The Bible Is the Inspired, Inerrant, and Authoritative Word of God
The parable affirms the truth that the Bible is the Word of God. It does
so in the title of the book Gildas is given: *The book of Arthur, High King
of Britain, written for the joy of all his noble subjects by Uther and
Yrgenus, the Royal Parents of the King, and with the faithful cooperation
of Merlin, servant of Arthur and sage of England.* The source of the book
is the royal family of Arthur. Merlin's part was one of "faithful cooperation" suggesting that, though he was involved in a meaningful way, he
is not the "author" of the book. Just as the Book of Arthur is the word of
the royal family of Britain, so the Bible is the word of the royal family
of all creation—the Trinity.

Yet to call the Bible the Word of God demands some further explanation. I'd like to look at three words that make clearer what the Christian
means when he affirms that the Bible is the word of God. Those three
words are *inspiration, inerrancy,* and *authority.*

Inspiration: The Origin of the Bible
What is inspiration? To answer that question we must distinguish between inspiration and revelation. God has revealed his will and ways
supremely in Jesus Christ. That is the heart of the idea behind special
revelation. But inspiration is different from revelation. Inspiration is the
process of recording revelation. Revelation is the original event or
manifestation of God. Christ himself and his saving acts are the heart of
God's self-disclosure. Scripture is the divinely created written record of
Christ's person and work. Inspiration makes it possible to claim that the
Bible is the Word of God.

I am always struck by the way in which the Bible speaks of itself as
the Word of God. Consider this small sampling of statements from
Scripture about its own identity:
☐ Habakkuk 2:2 —Then the LORD replied: "Write down the revelation
and make it plain on tablets so that a herald may run with it."
☐ Acts 4:25 —You [God] spoke by the Holy Spirit through the mouth of
your servant, our father David: "Why do the nations rage and the peoples
plot in vain?"
☐ Romans 3:1-2 —What advantage, then, is there in being a Jew, or what
value is there in circumcision? Much in every way! First of all, they have

been entrusted with the very words of God.

☐ 1 Thessalonians 2:13 —And we also thank God continually because, when you received the word of God, which you heard from us, you accepted it not as the word of men, but as it actually is, the word of God which is at work in you who believe.

Other verses could be mentioned that speak of the Bible as the "word of God," the "word of the Lord" and similar phrases. Hundreds of such references exist throughout the Bible. When we come to the Bible we come to a book that claims to be inspired, that is, to be the Word of God. "Every true Christian accepts the inspiration of the Bible in some sense," writes Bruce Milne. "The controversies center on *how* this inspiration occurred and on the implications of this for the authority and reliability of the actual words of Scripture as we now have them."[3]

What are some of the views that have been set forth on the inspiration of the Bible? Consider these five:

The *intuition theory* holds that the writers of the Bible were religious geniuses who had a high degree of insight into religious truth. In this view the writers of Scripture are essentially in the same category as Plato, Buddha and Muhammad. The emphasis here is on inspiration as a natural endowment possessed by an exceptional individual.

The *illumination theory* teaches that while the human authors of Scripture were responsible for the writing of Scripture, they were influenced by the Holy Spirit, who enhanced their natural powers. No special communication of truth occurred. This position has been held by some along the liberal part of the theological spectrum.

The *dynamic theory* maintains that the *thoughts* of the human writers are inspired by God, but not necessarily the actual words the authors chose to put down on paper. This helps explain the variety of styles found in the New Testament. The Baptist theologian A. H. Strong is a representative of this view.

The *verbal theory* holds that the Holy Spirit directed the human writers, even to the selection of the actual words in the text. The verbal theory also holds to the idea of confluence, by which the human authors freely chose the words they wrote but the Spirit so superintended the process that the result is the very written Word of God. Thus this view is distinguished from the so-called dictation view. This verbal view was the main view of historic Christianity and was ably articulated in the twentieth century by the Princeton theologian B. B. Warfield.

The *dictation theory* teaches that "God actually dictated the Bible to the writers." This view would ignore the role of the human authors in producing the Scripture. Millard Erickson warns that this has mistakenly been taken by liberals as the typical conservative view of inspiration. Evangelical theologians have taken pains to distinguish between dictation and verbal inspiration.[4]

How do we sort among these views and find the one that best suits what Scripture teaches? We need to take a closer look at three of the key texts before we select a view and explore it in more depth. Let us look more carefully at 2 Timothy 3:16, 2 Peter 1:20-21, and John 10:34-35.

Second Timothy 3:16 is perhaps the most famous text on inspiration for it is there that the word itself is found. The key phrase in the verse "All Scripture is God-breathed" (Theopneustos) points to the divine authorship of the Bible. "God's 'breath' is a familiar and graphic Old Testament metaphor for the action of God, particularly through his spirit (Gen 2:7; Job 33:4; Ps 33:6)."5 And what does God's Spirit produce? Writings. Scripture means writing. It is not just the writer's mind that is influenced nor just his soul that is moved. The passage completely ignores the human role in producing the Scriptures, for Paul wished to make a more important point. Words and written records were produced, and these came from the mouth of God. This characteristic of divine origin is true for all Scripture, i.e., all canonical writings. Thus Paul affirms in this passage that the whole of the Old Testament is the Word of God.

Second Peter 1:19-21 builds on Paul's statement in 2 Timothy. Peter talks of the eyewitness report his readers had of Christ and his saving acts. He then says that they have an authority for their teaching which is superior even to that of an eyewitness. That superior authority is the Word of God, the word of prophecy—here a reference to the Old Testament in general. How was the Old Testament produced so that it is so reliable, more reliable even than an eyewitness? Peter's bold answer is that, far from merely passing on the perceptions and opinions of men, the writers of the Old Testament spoke as they were "carried along by the Holy Spirit." In Acts 27:15, "carried along" (*pheromenoi*) describes a ship being driven along by a storm at sea. The word-picture seems clear. While men wrote the words that came to their mind, they were aware of and submitted themselves to the power of the Holy Spirit guiding their minds and hearts and pens and motivating them to write the very words of God. The final passage that illustrates and explains the nature of biblical inspiration is John 10:34-42. In this passage Jesus is discussing with his critics the phrase in Psalm 82, "You are gods." This can't be a mistake by the psalmist, says Jesus, because it is Scripture and "Scripture cannot be broken." Jesus thus affirms that the whole Old Testament is the Word of God and reveals his own high opinion of its inspiration.

From the above survey of passages I would like to suggest a definition of inspiration. Inspiration is that act of God the Holy Spirit by which he produced the written Word of God through the agency of human authors. Three words will help me explain this definition. I am suggesting, along with most evangelical theologians, that inspiration is verbal, plenary, and confluent.

Inspiration is *verbal.* The words of the text of Scripture are inspired, not just the writers themselves or the general ideas behind the writing. Second Timothy 3:16 makes this clear that all the written, canonical Scriptures are the product of the Spirit's divine work of production.

Inspiration is *plenary.* This means that the whole Bible from Genesis to Revelation is the Word of God. Against those who would recognize only parts of the Bible as inspired, the evangelical hears the Word of God teaching that "all Scripture is inspired." Some have argued that 2 Timothy 3:16 could be translated "All Scripture inspired by God is profitable." This reading would support the idea that there are two kinds of writing in the Bible—inspired and uninspired—and therefore would deny the idea that inspiration is plenary. Against this translation stand the normal rules of Greek grammar, which would identify the main subject as "Scripture" and the predicate as "inspired by God" and thus require that the verb "is" be placed between these terms.

Inspiration is *confluent.* What is meant by this rather clumsy word? The biblical doctrine of confluent inspiration teaches that God entered into partnership with human authors in the production of his Word. Both the word of humans and the word of God flowed together but in a way that God's intentions were fully realized while our participation was fully used. But surely, someone might object, if God controlled the human authors, then they were little more than stenographers taking down dictation. Aren't we sacrificing meaningful human involvement in the writing of the Bible with such a God-oriented view of inspiration? As Donald Bloesch complains, such a view of inspiration "can be faulted for underplaying the human element in the Bible."[6] I hear the complaint of Bloesch but have trouble agreeing with it. For me the doctrine of providence affirms that God is always behind the scenes as the ultimate cause of events. His general rule over life does not take away the human element of history—the responsible actions of men and women through time. I feel the same about the Bible. God can so shape the lives of his chosen human authors over the whole course of their personal history that when they come to that moment of actually writing down God's words, their whole being resonates to his inner prompting and their minds articulate exactly and with full consent the words suggested by the Spirit.

Inerrancy: The Accuracy of the Bible

Does inspiration demand inerrancy? Not all believers are sure. In the parable the title of the book speaks of Merlin's "faithful cooperation." This suggests that what the royal family wanted to say, Merlin reliably conveyed. Yet Sister Charis was not so sure: "Probably filled with bunk even if the main accounts are right." What are we to think about inerrancy?

My first concern is to listen to what Scripture says about itself. I hear its clear testimony to be the written Word of God. Does it also testify that it is free from error? Consider the following verses:

☐ Psalm 12:6—And the words of the LORD are flawless, like silver refined in a furnace of clay, purified seven times.

☐ Psalm 18:30—As for God, his way is perfect; the word of the LORD is flawless.[7]

☐ Psalm 119:89—Your word, O LORD, is eternal; it stands firm in the heavens.

☐ Proverbs 30:5-6—Every word of God is flawless; he is a shield to those who take refuge in him. Do not add to his words, or he will rebuke you and prove you a liar.

☐ John 10:35—The Scripture cannot be broken.

Are these not clear testimonies of the Bible's own self-understanding? I read them and conclude that inerrancy, or freedom from falsehood and deception, is a characteristic of the inspired text of Scripture.

But are there not different ways of understanding the truthfulness of the Bible and words such as *inerrancy* and *infallibility*? Let's look at a few of these different views on the issue.

One view is that of scientific inerrancy. This view tends to assert that the Bible is inerrant in a strict scientific sense. Whatever the current canons of scientific and historical accuracy may be, the Bible, it is purported, will meet these. Thus Harold Lindsell in his *Battle for the Bible* deals with the apparent discrepancy in 2 Chronicles 4:2, which says the molten sea built as part of the worship at the temple was ten cubits in diameter and thirty cubits in its circumference. But to find the circumference of a circle, as every teenager studying geometry knows (though I admit I had to brush up on this bit of math!), you must multiply the diameter (in this case 10) by 3.14159 (the value of π). This would yield more than thirty cubits. Has the Bible committed an error? A good deal of space in Lindsell's book is spent harmonizing this apparent discrepancy. The days of Genesis 1, the statement by Christ about the mustard seed being the smallest of the seeds (which I am told it is not)—all require careful explanation to ensure that they meet the canons of scientific accuracy and exactness.[8]

A second view is full inerrancy. The Bible is completely truthful in all areas, including matters of science and history. Like scientific inerrancy, this position affirms the total infallibility of the Bible in matters of faith. But unlike the absolute inerrancy position, full inerrancy does not demand that contemporary science be the standard for accuracy. Biblical descriptions of matters of science and history are popular descriptions. They are correct and without error given the "man-in-the-street" perspective from which the biblical authors wrote.

A third view is limited inerrancy. The Bible is inerrant in matters of faith and salvation, but it contains errors of fact in the areas of science and history. Biblical writers were people of their day and thus subject to the limited knowledge characteristic of the day. This view would accord with the statement that the Bible inerrantly and infallibly fulfills its intended purpose of bringing men and women to salvation through Christ but would not extend inerrancy much beyond that.

A fourth view is that of full errancy. This view does not teach that the Bible is totally in error but that everything the Bible teaches or contains is capable of error. This view, then, abandons the idea of inerrancy and holds that since the Bible had human authors, human error must have crept into the text. Paul was wrong on his view of women, or had two or three incompatible views of the resurrection. There is no need to harmonize because there is no need to defend inerrancy. The Bible may or may not be the Word of God in this view. It is so completely a human book that it may err, not only in matters of science and history, but in matters of theology and ethics as well.

For a number of reasons, I am compelled to accept the term inerrancy as an important part of a truly Christian perspective on Scripture. The full inerrancy view seems most in keeping with both the nature of Scripture and the need to resist the temptation to accept modern standards of scientific measurement and historical accuracy as the absolute tests of truth. A commonsense description of a rocket launch at Cape Kennedy is just as "true" as a rocket scientist's more technical description. The one description is in terms of "what I saw," and the other is in terms of mathematics and physics. Scripture uses language of the first kind, the language of common perception. God speaks in "baby talk" to us there, as Calvin said.

The inspired Word of God comes draped in human language and everyday descriptions. It is fully inerrant in all that it affirms, not full of bunk as Sister Charis complained. But its sublimity is not found in its ability to satisfy scientific standards of accuracy developed nearly two thousand years after the completion of its writing. Its beauty is "of a different sort: Miles deeper and further in."

Authority: The Power of the Bible

In light of the doctrine of the Bible presented above, we must conclude that it has absolute authority to command obedience and belief because it is the Word of God. God as Creator of all reality and Lord of history has already interpreted everything. Truth is whatever God says it is. Hebrews 6:13-18 captures the character of biblical authority well. It refers to an Old Testament episode in Genesis 22:16-18 ("I swear by myself," v. 16) when God swore by his own name that he would give Abraham the promised son:

> When God made his promise to Abraham, since there was no one greater for him to swear by, he swore by himself, saying, "I will surely bless you and give you many descendants." And so after waiting patiently, Abraham received what was promised.

> Men swear by someone greater than themselves, and the oath confirms what is said and puts an end to all argument. Because God wanted to make the unchanging nature of his purpose very clear, . . . he confirmed it with an oath. God did this so that, by two unchangeable things in which it is impossible for God to lie, we . . . may be greatly encouraged.

This is the great principle of truth: The Bible cannot lie, because it is the word of the great God who cannot lie. God cannot lie, because he is omniscient and holy. Thus the Bible's perspective on anything represents the normative perspective (not the only perspective) on anything. But note something else about the truth of the Bible. Since it is God's word, it can be judged only by itself. In other words, the authority of the Bible is self-authenticating. It cannot be judged by any lesser authority without committing intellectual rebellion against God. Since the Bible is the Word of God, only the Bible can confirm the Bible.

Each of the rival views of authority brings a certain unquestioned assumption about reality when their proponents sit down to decide whether they will accept something as true. A rationalist brings a basic belief such as "I think, therefore I am," which some people go on to use as a foundation for "What I choose to think about things is the real test of truth" (until I'm shown otherwise). The egoist brings the assumption that "I am the center of the universe and truth is whatever liberates me to reach my potential." The fan of modernity brings the assumption that "whatever is fashionable is true." And so on down the line.

Do you see the common assumption with which every rival authority begins its search for truth and reliable knowledge? Beneath all of the stated assumptions is the ultimate presupposition that "the God of the Bible does not exist" or that "the God of the Bible has not spoken." Every rival authority judges the Bible by beginning with rebellious presuppositions that the Bible is not self-authenticating because the God of the

Bible is not the basis of all reality and truth.

But the Christian looks at truth in a very different way. She begins with the most basic assumption of all: that the Triune God of the Bible exists. There is no "truth" or fact in the universe that has the right to judge that statement. To do so would mean that she allowed something other than the Triune God to be the ultimate truth, the primary authority in her life. Beginning with the ultimate truth of the Triune God, who speaks in the Scriptures, I come to a world already interpreted by him. This is the foundation for certain and reliable knowledge in every field. By accepting the authority of the Bible as the self-authenticating word of the Triune God, I know the ultimate truths about life and also have a foundation for rationality—thinking God's thoughts after him.

The Bible's Purpose Is to Increase Our Delight in God

All that I have said thus far will head us in the wrong direction if we do not follow Gildas and Galahad all the way and recognize that the purpose of the book is to cultivate and increase our joy in our King. Remember our definition of theology: the art and science of enjoying God through Christ in all of life. We need to make sure our theology of the Bible is focused in this direction. Consider three ways we can use the Bible to increase our joy in God.

First, we can increase our delight in God by rekindling flagging desire through meditation on the Bible. John Piper strikes a realistic note about Christian hedonism when he admits that those who seek their delight in God sometimes experience anything but:

> Christian Hedonism is much aware that every day with Jesus is *not* "sweeter than the day before." Some days with Jesus our disposition is sour. Some days with Jesus are so sad we feel our heart will break open. Some days with Jesus are so depressed and discouraged that between the garage and the house we just want to sit down on the grass and cry.[9]

But it is precisely at such moments that the power of the Word of God to restore our joy is so appreciated. "The law of the LORD is perfect, reviving the soul," says Psalm 19:7. Piper responds to David's statement in Psalm 19: "Even on days when every cinder in our soul feels cold, if we crawl to the Word of God and cry out for ears to hear, the cold ashes will be lifted and the tiny spark of life will be fanned."[10]

The Bible rekindles flagging desire for God.

Second, we can increase our joyful confidence in God through the renewal of biblical preaching and teaching. In 1 Corinthians 1:21 Paul admits that preaching sometimes appears foolish, not so much because of the process itself (good orators always get a crowd) but because of what was preached—the convicting Word of God. The Bible's message of creation, fall, and redemption is a message that meets resistance in the human heart. My fallen heart will run from the book that reminds me of these things and conspire with the pulpit of my church to blunt their force or speak these truths as though they were human ideas (and therefore negotiable) and not the very words of God.

But if I am called to preach or teach, I can do no greater service to the spiritual health of my people than engage in biblical preaching or teaching. By "biblical preaching" I mean the preaching that is born of serious study and prayer over the text, rises in clear explanation of the text from the pulpit and culminates in sensitive application of the text to the lives of the congregation. Such preaching is a great service in increasing our joyful confidence in God, because "nothing is more calculated to bring renewal of the life, vigor and faith of the church in any generation than the unleashing of God's everlasting Word in the midst of his people through the ministry of expositor-preachers anointed by his Holy Spirit."[11]

Third, we can increase our glad submission to God by applying the Bible's truths to all of life.

"Thy word," David confesses with gladness, "is a lamp unto my feet and a light unto my path" (Ps 119:105 KJV). The Bible sheds light on every path of life, not just "spiritual" paths. The engineer, the politician, the plumber, and the mathematician all need the Word of God to do their work obediently and not rebelliously. The engineer, only through the renewal of his mind by the Word and the Spirit, will see the drawing of blueprints not just as a bare act of drawing blueprints but as a covenant act of drawing God's blueprints, an action that God wants done in his way and for his glory.

The Bible does not necessarily tell us the structural or creational norms that must be applied to draw good blueprints. These kinds of norms are learned through the study of God's general revelation in creation and culture. That's why we go to school or do internships. Structural norms are typically passed on in that way. But the Bible gives me lots of directional norms that tell me how to do any action for God and not for idols. It can change my heart and redirect it from the inevitable moral and religious corruption that comes into every action done by fallen people in a fallen world.

The Bible will not change the norms of algebra the mathematician uses each day, but it can give her a new awareness that she is using not an autonomous algebra but a God-originated and God-owned algebra, and she can thus act not as an autonomous mathematician but as a covenantal mathematician. Every area of life can enjoy renewed direction when the Bible is applied to that sphere.

Conclusion

Into a miserable life in decline *The Book of Arthur* brought joy and renewal. This is the promise of the Bible for our world. The parable sought to increase our understanding and appreciation of this remarkable book by making three affirmations: The Bible is revelation from God; the Bible is the inspired, inerrant and authoritative Word of God; and the Bible's purpose is to increase our joy in God.

When these ideas become part of our worldview, the words of Psalm 19:8, 10-11 will make delightful sense:

The precepts of the LORD are right, giving joy to the heart. . . . They are more precious than gold, than much pure gold; they are sweeter than honey, than honey from the comb. By them is your servant warned; in keeping them there is great reward.

Questions for Individuals or for Group Discussion

Part One

1. The title of the book given to Gildas is *The book of Arthur, High King of Britain, written for the joy of all his noble subjects by Uther and Yrgenus, the Royal Parents of the King, and with the faithful cooperation of Merlin, servant of Arthur and sage of England.* What does this title suggest about the following:

a. the theme of the Bible (cf. 2 Tim 3:15; Lk 24:25-27)?

b. the inspiration of the Bible and the way the divine and human authors relate?

c. the inerrancy of Scripture?

2. What is Sir Gawain's criticism of the *Book of Arthur?*
What do you think is behind that criticism?
Who would give this kind of criticism today?

3. What is Father Geoffrey's criticism?
Who would give this kind of criticism today?

4. What is Sister Charis's criticism?
Who would give this kind of criticism today?

5. What is the reaction of Gildas to these criticisms? Why?
What are some of the symptoms of contemporary believers' discouragement with the Scriptures?

6. What were the benefits of the Book of Arthur in the lives of Gildas and Galahad?
In what ways does the Bible make a similar impact in the lives of those who follow Christ?
Can it really "communicate Christ's presence and power"? How does that happen?

Part Two

7. Which of the attacks on the Bible carries the most sting for you personally: rationalism, traditionalism, or higher criticism?
Are there any others not mentioned?

8. Does general revelation make it possible for non-Christian religions to find God? Why or why not?

9. How does the view of inspiration advocated here do justice to the human role in creating the Bible?

10. What are the reasons given in the comment for asserting the Bible's authority?
What is meant by saying that the Bible is "self-authenticating"?

11. Of the various ways the Bible can restore our joy in God, which ones speak to you personally with the most force?
What additional values and benefits of the Bible can you mention that are neglected in the "Theology Behind the Story" section?

12. What's the idea behind the idea of "covenant algebra"? Do you

agree or disagree?

For Further Reading
Though written in the 1950s, J. I. Packer's *Fundamentalism and the Word of God* (Grand Rapids: Eerdmans, 1958) is still one of the best brief defenses of the evangelical doctrine of Scripture available. Two more recent evangelical responses to critics of biblical authority are D. A. Carson and J. D. Woodbridge, eds., *Scripture and Truth* (Grand Rapids: Zondervan, 1983); and John J. Davis, *Foundations of Evangelical Theology* (Grand Rapids: Baker, 1984).

Chapter Three
The Trinity:
The Pride of Simba

T*here is a place in African* folklore called the land of Simba. If you are young enough (either in age or in heart) and brave enough you might be able to find this enchanted place. To find it you must head straight toward the Mountains of the Moon and then take a left at the Nile and count to ten in Swahili with your eyes closed. If the legends are true, then when you open your eyes you will be in the land of Simba. Simba was, according to the ancient tales, the son of the great Lion-Lord who created Africa. When sin and selfishness came to the continent, and death and wickedness began to ruin his good creation, the Lion-Lord (revered as the Creator God) took pity on his creatures (although they did not deserve it) and came down to earth in the form of a lion. Simba was killed by those he came to deliver, but his death cleansed the earth of evil. Legend speaks of how Simba rose from death and created this new and enchanted place—the land of Simba—as a refuge to all who were in need.

Once upon a time four children, whose village was ravaged by a terrible famine, decided to find the land of Simba and to ask the great Lion to give them food to take back to their starving people. All the people of the village worshiped Simba and were troubled that he did not seem to hear and answer their prayers. Had he not died to deliver them from just this sort of suffering? The children were convinced that if they could just talk to the Lion in person, all would be well and the prayers of the village would be answered.

Like little crusaders marching to fight the infidel, they left their home early one morning (leaving a note behind) and made their way toward the Mountains of the Moon. They took a left at the Nile. They stopped and closed their eyes.

They counted to ten in Swahili. When they opened their eyes (very slowly), to their wonder and surprise they found themselves in a place of great enchantment and beauty. The horrors of the deadly drought were gone, and green and blue and gold ran over the landscape like colors spilled from an artist's palette. Streams of bright and clear water glided through the flower-covered meadows. The children ran and played as carefree as the plume of snow that blew off the high peaks of the Mountains of the Moon.

I should tell you the names of these children. The older two were Mvula and Grace. The younger two were Mumo and Wanjari. They were brothers and sisters, and they got along well with one another (most of the time).

The four children began to explore this new place (which they were sure was the land of Simba), and after several hours found a stand of mango trees, their branches bending with plump fruit. Mvula told the others to join him in gathering up the mangos, for this would be the food that would save their village. Wanjari and Grace had brought some bright-colored cloth with them that the African people call *kangas*. The plan was to eat a few mangos themselves and then fill the kangas with as many mangos as they could carry and return immediately to their hungry village.

But Mumo had other plans. Instead of eating a mango or two and then filling the kanga with mangos for the village, Mumo just kept eating. He even took some of the plump mangos that Wanjari had placed in her kanga and began eating them.

"Those mangos are for the village, not for you," Wanjari said to Mumo. "If Simba saw what you are doing, he would not be pleased."

"Simba wouldn't mind. After all, weren't we taught that Simba does every-thing for his own glory—in other words, for himself? If he is totally self-cen-tered and we are followers of Simba, then we have a right to put ourselves first," said Mumo as he grabbed another mango from Wanjari's pile.

"You shouldn't talk that way about Simba," Wanjari said, more loudly than she intended. "Simba is not selfish. Isn't he the one who created our land and died for us and rose again to make it all new? How could you call him self-centered?"

Mumo sneered at Wanjari and said something that made her eyes grow wide and fill with tears. "I have been thinking about why the Simba that we worship did all of these things, and I have come to two possible conclusions. He did it either because he was lonely and needed creatures to keep him company or because he was greedy for more glory. Either way, Simba the magnificent is completely self-centered. And if he is, then I figure I'm in good company."

Wanjari, still sniffling, said, "That's not true, Mumo. Simba created us and died for us and our land because he loved us. That is his motive."

"But what kind of love moved him to die, Wanjari? The only kind of love he has is self-love, because if he saved us either to stop being lonely or to glorify himself, it was still selfishness and self-love all the same." And with that Mumo grabbed another of his sister's mangos and then kicked over the rest of her carefully made pile.

Wanjari began to cry so loudly that the two older children came running from the other side of the orchard. Just as they were about to ask what was wrong, they heard the most terrifying roar that they had ever heard. A huge shadow swept across the orchard. The four children looked up at the hill above the orchard. Standing on the hill and rimmed with light was a lion of such magnificence that they all knew it must be Simba himself.

Mumo's face was hot with shame and dread. Simba, after all, was a lion, not a kitten. He was powerful and he was wild. Cowering before the Creator Beast of the land around them (as well as all other lands), Mumo wondered if his next breath would be his last.

Just then a strange thing happened. Simba raised his head and opened his mouth wide. His huge teeth sparkled in the sunlight. Mumo plugged his ears, waiting for the deafening roar of wrath which could crack rocks wide open. But instead of a thunderous roar, the children heard only a hearty and lusty laugh. Simba was laughing, and his laugh was like a waterfall of music, each note tickling the other until it created a riot of joyous sound. Winds carried it for miles, the sun glowed more intensely in its beauty, and the trees swayed with waving green as though applauding the lion.

"Son of Africa," said Simba, looking directly at Mumo, "so you think you have discovered my deepest motives and have been able to unravel the mystery of my love for you and this realm? 'He did it either because he was lonely and needed creatures to keep him company or because he was greedy for more glory. Either way Simba the magnificent is completely self-centered.' I believe that is what you said."

Mumo wanted to run but knew that he could not outrun Simba. He was frozen with fear.

"Jump on my back, each of you," commanded the great Lion. Grace and Mvula slowly climbed onto the massive back of the Lion. Wanjari was next. Mumo was last.

"Hold onto my mane," said Simba when they were all on. In an instant Simba bounded off. The children felt the wind whipping over them three times more forcefully than if they had been seated on the swiftest bird in Africa.

Within minutes they found themselves on top of a high cliff overlooking the

Nile. It was called Pride Point ("pride" being the name for a lion family) and was a place of deep magic. In the middle of the high meadow that made up Pride Point was a statue, actually four statues, that gave the point its name. There before the children (who had rolled off the Lion's back and had landed softly in the warm but still wet grass) were the marble figures of four colossal lions, one in the center and three making a circle around it.

"Who are the four lions?" asked Mvula.

"There are not four lions," answered Simba. "There are three lions and one Lion-Lord. The three lions are the one Lion-Lord."

"Oh, yes, I see," said Mvula, but of course he did not see at all.

"I beg your pardon, Simba," Grace said, with a slight tremble in her voice, "but I don't think I understand what you mean."

Now Simba roared till the whole meadow shook. But it was not a roar of anger or irritation. It was more a roar of excitement and, perhaps, joy. "I am a member of a pride of lions," explained Simba, licking away the dryness around his mouth from his roar. "My Father, the great one on the Nile side of the circle, is called Lion-Father. The lion on the east side of the circle is my brother, Lionheart. And I am the statue on the south side of the circle.

"We have been a pride before time began and will remain a pride when time is no more. We live to love, exalt and enjoy the other members of the pride, and everything we do and say is for the good pleasure of the other. The creation of Africa, my death to save it, and my building of this enchanted kingdom are all the joint works of Lion-Father, Lionheart, and me done to show our love and joy in one another and not ourselves. Some kind of self-love, eh, Mumo?"

Mumo said nothing and kept his face fixed on the four statues.

"But what about the lion in the middle?" asked Wanjari with genuine confusion.

"The middle statue is the One Lion-Lord, without limits, without divisions and full to overflowing with a love that fills the world," answered Simba.

"But that still adds up to four lions," insisted Grace and Mvula, who had done a little math at school.

"No," said the great Lion firmly. "Our pride of three is a Lord of one. We are three and one at the same time. It is equally true to say that the Lion-Lord is a pride and to say that he is one. Neither truth is complete without the other."

The children looked more confused than ever.

Simba gathered them into his paws and looked deep into their eyes. He felt warm and gentle to the children. "I am the one Lion-Lord and also the second member of the pride. Lion-Father is the one Lion-Lord and the first member of the pride. Lionheart is the one Lion-Lord and the third and final member of the pride. I am the one Lion-Lord without beginning and end, creator and sustainer of all things. No one created me. I am self-existent (just as Lion-Father and Lionheart are). At the same time, I am the male cub of my father freely receiving life from him without beginning or end."

Mvula interrupted Simba. "But what about Lionheart? How does he fit into the pride?"

"Lionheart is the one Lion-Lord, who has (like Lion-Father and me) the fullness of Lionlordship within himself," Simba said. "Both Lion-Father and I have given life to Lionheart from before time began. He has a very special role. When I want to express my love and delight and honor to my Father, I go to Lionheart and pour my heart out to him. Filled with my joy and love, Lionheart goes to my Father and fills his heart with delight by sharing my love with him. Is that all he does, you may wonder? No, he does something even more wonderful. Lion-Father tells Lionheart of his delight and love for me. He gets all filled up again with new joy and brings it to me. That's what he lives to do—he lives to honor and exalt and delight in Lion-Father and me by acting as the go-between of our love for one another. Because he fills that role as go-between with such glad submission, we in turn are full of love for him and desire to honor, enjoy and serve him."

Grace spoke up. "This is still a puzzle to me with all this oneness and threeness going on at the same time. What I am beginning to understand is that the Lion-Lord is like nothing else in the land of Simba; that he is but one Lion-Lord over all things; that he is also and equally a pride of three, Lion-Father, Lionheart and yourself; and that your love is not self-love but is family-centered love. That means that you didn't need to make Africa, or die for us, or make things new again to be loving or overcome loneliness. You were loving within the pride before time began. Your love has always been unselfish and always full."

Simba stood to full height and laid his giant paw on Grace's head. "Daughter of Africa, you have learned much about the family life of Simba today. What do you think of Grace's ideas, Mumo?" the lion asked, turning his head toward the boy still lying in the grass.

"I-I-I think I owe you an apology, Sir," Mumo said slowly and with a stutter. "But if you did not create us out of loneliness or selfishness, then why did you do it?"

"You will not be able to understand me," said Simba, kneeling close to Mumo now and almost whispering to him, "just by looking at these statues and hearing someone talk. When you see our pride in action, you can understand more about why we do what we do and what kind of love motivates us."

Wanjari jumped up at that point and began to shout, "And so that's why you made our land and permitted it to fall and why you came to die. You were showing both what your one Lionlordship was like and what the relationship of the members of the pride was like!"

Mvula interrupted. "Does that mean, Simba, that the whole pride was involved in some way in the creation of Africa and its restoration in order to act out—or even celebrate—the life that you've enjoyed eternally within the pride with all of your love and exalting and serving one another?"

Simba did not answer. The great Lion just purred, and after Mvula, Grace, Wanjari and Mumo climbed up on his back, they began the return journey to the orchard. Mumo glanced back at the statues just before they were out of sight and could have sworn that he saw a smile dance across their faces.

The Theology Behind the Story: **The Trinity**

God is love because he is Trinity. That is the bold idea of this parable. But what is meant by such a statement? How puzzling it must sound to some of us. The problem is not that we *reject* the doctrine of the Trinity. Rather, the problem is that we often *neglect* the doctrine of the Trinity. This neglect is fairly recent. There was a time that evangelicals called the doctrine of the Trinity "the foundation of all our communion with God, and comfortable dependence on him."[1] I'm not sure we feel that way anymore. Yet the Word of God, which discloses God to us, has shown him to be one God in three persons, Father, Son, and Holy Spirit. If we take the Bible seriously, we must take the Trinity seriously. And as our ancestors felt, there are important consequences in taking the Trinity seriously. "Communion with God" and "comfortable dependence" on God may richly flow from a fresh rediscovery of God as Trinity.

So I repeat the statement: God is love because he is Trinity. I would like to get inside that statement and unpack its meaning by looking at three affirmations drawn from the parable and ultimately based on Scripture. I hope that Grace's discovery at the end of the parable will be our own: "You were loving within the pride before time began. Your love has always been unselfish and always full."

God Is Love Because He Is Trinity
In the parable, Mumo brought tears to his sister's eyes by accusing Simba

of harboring a selfish love. Have you ever wondered how God can be loving and yet still make all these statements about seeking his own glory? We certainly don't like people who are that way. How can we really like a God who would be that way? I think we need to talk a little about the different kinds of love and particularly the way God loves. The doctrine of the Trinity answers the kind of objection the Mumos of the world (or in our own hearts) might make about God and his love.

I believe that God's love is anything but selfish or human-centered. In contrast to both misunderstandings about God, the Bible roots the love of God in the truth of the Trinity. Simba, in the parable, summarizes in a few key sentences what I believe to be the biblical teaching on love within the Trinity:

> We live to love, exalt and enjoy the other members of the pride, and everything we do and say is for the good pleasure of the other. The creation of Africa, my death to save it, and my building of this enchanted kingdom are all joint works of Lion-Father, Lionheart, and me done to show our love and joy in one another and not ourselves. Some kind of self-love, eh, Mumo?

Are these really biblical ideas? We need to look at that question and consider the biblical witness to the Trinity. First of all, the whole Bible (and not just the New Testament) presents God as Trinity. Consider the following points that present the truth of the Trinity as it unfolds in Scripture.

(1) God is one (Deut 6:4). Bruce Milne writes that "this insistence on the divine unity was most important because of the idolatrous, depraved polytheism of the surrounding nations."[2]

(2) There is a plurality and "fullness" in God's oneness (Gen 1:26; 3:22; 11:7; Is 6:8; cf. Jn 12:41). *Elohim* in Genesis 1:26 is a rich word. It is found in the plural when it refers to the God of Israel. While some scholars see the grammatical construction as a "plural of majesty," other scholars have argued that it is a "quantitative plural," meaning that it is intended to convey diversity in unity.[3]

(3) The Father is God (Mt 6:8; 7:21; Gal 1:1). The deity of the Father is uncontested.

(4) The Son is God (Jn 1:1-18; Rom 9:5; Col 2:9; Tit 2:13; Heb 1:8-10). The Son is called by divine names, possesses divine attributes and

performs deeds appropriate only to God.

(5) The Spirit is God (Mk 3:29; Jn 15:26; 1 Cor 6:19; 2 Cor 3:17). Every way in which the Son's deity is affirmed, so too is the Spirit's deity affirmed.

(6) The three persons are one God (Mt 3:13-17; 28:19; Acts 2:32ff.; 2 Cor 13:14; Eph 1:1-14; 3:16-19). We are to be baptized in the "name" (not "names") of the Father, Son and Spirit.

The conclusion we draw from these witnesses is simple. The one God is also a plurality of persons. The Father is God, the Son is God, and the Spirit is God; but we do not have three Gods, for the Bible insists that God is one. The doctrine of the Trinity is the logical combination of all these clear assertions about God. Although the word *Trinity* is not found in the Bible and was not coined until the second century (by Tertullian), it accurately captures the combined teaching of Scripture. Our God is triune.

All this is plain enough for the person who accepts Scripture's authority. But is that all the Bible says about the Trinity? What about Simba's statement that we "live to love, exalt and enjoy the other members of the pride, and everything we do and say is for the good pleasure of the other"? Where do we find that in the Word of God?

The love among the persons of the Trinity is displayed very clearly in the Gospel of John. I'd like to focus on the fuller portrait of the triune God painted in the fourth Gospel and peer more deeply into this mystery of the Trinity. We could look at virtually every chapter of John, but we will limit our survey to a few key chapters. Note in particular how each chapter affirms four things about either the Father and the Son or all three members of the Trinity: (1) their full equality, (2) their glad submission to one another, (3) their enjoyment of intimacy with one another and (4) their mutual deference.

In John 1:1 the Father and the Son are declared to be equals, for the "Word was with God, and the Word was God." Although enjoying a relationship of full equality, the Word, in glad submission, "became flesh and made his dwelling among us" (v. 14). The Word seeks to honor and exalt the Father by making him known (v. 18). And he has enjoyed intimacy with the Father because "no one has ever seen God, but God the One and Only, who is at the Father's side" (v. 18).

In the third chapter of John the evangelist shows that the glad submission and deference of the Son to the Father (v. 34: "the one whom God has sent speaks the words of God") is also reciprocal. Verse 35 goes on to state: "The Father loves the Son and has placed everything in his hands."

In John 5 we see equality, submission, deference and intimacy at work again. Christ is criticized for "calling God his own Father, making himself equal with God" (v. 18). Mutual deference is described in verses 22-23: "The Father judges no one, but has entrusted all judgment to the Son, that all may honor the Son just as they honor the Father. He who does not honor the Son does not honor the Father, who sent him." Mutual submission is seen in verses 36-37: "I have testimony weightier than that of John. For the very work that the Father has given me to finish, and which I am doing, testifies that the Father has sent me." Mutual witness is the face of mutual submission. The intimate delight between Father and Son is found in verse 20 with its bold statement that the "Father loves the Son."

Notice how these four themes flow through John 8. Equality: "If you knew me, you would know my Father also" (v. 19) and "before Abraham was born, I am" (v. 58). Deference of the Son to the Father: "I am not possessed by a demon, . . . but I honor my Father" (v. 49). Deference of the Father to the Son: "If I glorify myself, my glory means nothing. My Father, whom you claim as your God, is the one who glorifies me" (v. 54). Intimacy: "I do know him [the Father] and keep his word" (v. 55). Glad submission: "The one who sent me is with me; he has not left me alone, for I always do what pleases him" (v. 29).

John 10 is filled with testimonies to this agapic relationship between the Father and the Son. Intimacy is clear in verse 17: "The reason my Father loves me is that I lay down my life." An astonishing claim to intimacy and equality is made in verse 30, "I and the Father are one," and again in verse 38: "the Father is in me, and I in the Father." He submits to the Father by having shown "many great miracles from the Father" (v. 32). Mutual deference is displayed in the Father empowering the Son and the Son wielding power under the Father's authority as he contemplates his impending death in verse 18: "No one takes it [my life] from me, but I lay it down of my own accord. I have authority to lay it down and authority to take it up again. This command I received from my Father."

In John 14 this relationship of intimacy, equality, honor and submission between Father and Son is now shared with a third person—the Holy Spirit: "And I will ask the Father, and he will give you another Counselor, to be with you forever—the Spirit of Truth. The world cannot accept him, because it neither sees him nor knows him. But you know him, for he lives with you and will be in you" (vv. 16-17). This is a relationship of equality, for the Spirit is "another" Counselor—not another kind of Counselor, but another of the same kind, meaning that whatever Christ is in essence, so also is the Spirit.

John 16 and 17 deepen this picture of the divine family at work to love, exalt, enjoy, and serve one another by loving, exalting, enjoying, and serving redeemed sinners. God is love because he is Trinity (a divine family of mutual love, service, delight, and equality), and his love for us is the sharing of this family love and no other.

In light of this evidence from John, we begin to understand that a new kind of love has appeared. We now can have a sharper understanding of what it means to say that God is love. It does not mean primarily that he is love because he loves us. Nor does it mean that he is love because he loves the nations. Such a view of God's love ends up making God dependent on humanity. God is love independent of anything in creation. Rather, to say that God is love is to say that the Father and Son and the Spirit live to enjoy, honor, and serve one another eternally. This God-centered love between the members of the Trinity, often called *agapē* in the New Testament, is the motive behind creation and redemption. This is the first love of all loves and is the source of all other loves. Simba was right and Mumo was wrong. The One who is Three lives to love, exalt, and enjoy the other members of this divine family. Such a God is to be richly enjoyed by his people.

Orthodox Understanding

Simba tried to explain to the children (with some difficulty) the nature of the pride to which he belonged. Do you remember what he said?

I am the one Lion-Lord and also the second member of the pride. Lion-Father is the one Lion-Lord and the first member of the pride. Lionheart is the one Lion-Lord and the third and final member of the pride. I am the one Lion-Lord without beginning and end, creator and sustainer of all things. No one created me. I am self-existent (just as Lion-Father and Lionheart are). At the same time, I am the male cub of my Father freely receiving life from him without beginning or end. The history of the Christian church illustrates both how thrilling and how difficult it has been to hold on to this God-centered view of the Trinity. I am convinced that one's value system, one's view of love, shapes one's concept of the Trinity. In other words, our values are expressed in creeds and theological statements. The twists and turns of historical theology have only deepened my conviction that theology is really a glimpse into the heart.

The Arian controversy of the fourth century was one of the most important theological battles that the Christian church has ever fought. The orthodox doctrine of the Trinity was the result. I would like to discuss how the biblical picture of the divine family was forged through that controversy.

We begin in Africa. African theology played a critical role in the church's thinking about God. Tertullian (from Carthage in North Africa; he died approximately A.D. 212) contributed to the preaching and teaching of the church of his day by maintaining the family (and agapic) character of God: "God is one in essence but three in person." Tertullian understood *person* not in the modern sense of isolated individual, but rather as relational quality (capable of relationship). He argued that the persons in the Trinity cannot be divided (as the Greek gods of the divine pantheon had), but can be distinguished. Thus was born the basic terminology with which the church would preserve and deepen the biblical portrait of God. It was a classic moment in the history of theology. But it didn't last long.

Origen of Alexandria, the brilliant exegete, thought he would lend his impressive intellect to the discussion of God. And as other brilliant and well-meaning intellectuals have discovered since, his contributions caused confusion. The Logos, taught Origen, was true God in most ways, but in some ways essentially subordinate to God. The Son was a "species" of God. The Holy Spirit's divine status was even shakier. For Origen the Spirit was a creature. It is to Origen that we owe the major headache of trinitarian semantics: he introduced the confusing language of one *ousia* in three *hypostases* (both words had originally meant pretty much the same thing—the essential nature of a thing). Though most people had regarded these two words as synonyms, they now were employed in new and confusing ways. There was more than a little head scratching in the Greek-speaking East as well as the Latin-speaking West. The head scratching turned into a migraine in A.D. 325 with the Arian controversy.

One attempt to clear up the ambiguities left by Origen was Arianism. This clarification of the doctrine of God represents one of the major ideological blow-ups in Western civilization. Arius's leading idea was that since God is an unbegotten, unoriginated being, if he has a begotten Son, that Son cannot be God. Therefore, the incarnate Logos must be a creature. He made the church authorities squirm by quoting troublesome texts (Prov 8:22; Mk 13:32; Lk 18:19; 1 Cor 15:28). Arians of the fourth century and those of the twentieth (such as Jehovah's Witnesses) have been quick to pounce on such verses and employ them for their argument against orthodoxy.[4] In A.D. 318 Arius was boldly teaching Alexandrian Christians that the Son was "alien from and utterly dissimilar (*anomoios*) to the Father's substance (*ousia*)," but he put this in more persuasive language and popular music and had it sung from church to church. The Father, Son, and Spirit do not share a single nature, said Arius and his entourage, but are not three separate Gods. The Son and Spirit are created beings. It was one way to counterattack Sabellianism (which taught that God is one essential being in three successive forms). It was radically different from Tertullian's solution, however. Arianism swept the churches of the fourth century like the desert winds that howled across North Africa.

What might come from Arius's views? For one, if you deny that Christ is God and confess that Christ is a creature, even one who is glorious and Godlike, then you open the door for our own ascent to God through personal moral achievement. The cross becomes less an atonement for sin and more a display of an extreme obedience that we can emulate, and so we can earn an exalted standing with God just as Christ did. Classic agapic love was being pushed aside by the Arians in this debate over the Trinity.

The most effective opposition to Arianism came from Athanasius (who died A.D. 373), who after the death of Alexander of Alexandria become the bishop of the city. This clear-sighted champion of orthodoxy fought long and eloquently for a full trinitarian doctrine of God against all subordinationist views of Christ. Driving Athanasius was a heart for the gospel: if Christ is not truly the God-man, then the cross is not complete redemption, for an inferior mediator is involved. A mediated reconciliation between two enemies is only as good as the mediator who accomplishes it. If there is any room for one or both of the parties to argue that they were not perfectly represented, then the deal can crumble. He was determined that such an unraveling of the gospel by Arian hanky-panky would not occur.

The church at large was soon caught up in this bitter argument and a council was called in 325 (with a little arm twisting by the new Christian emperor, Constantine) to settle the debate. The decision of those who gathered in Nicea (in modern-day Turkey) was as follows:

> We believe in one God, the Father almighty, maker of all things, visible and invisible; and in one Lord Jesus Christ, the Son of God, begotten from the Father, only-begotten, that is, from the substance of the Father, God from God, Light from Light, True God from True God, begotten not made, of one substance with the Father, through whom all things came into being, things in heaven and things on earth; Who because of us men and because of our salvation, came down and became incarnate, becoming man, suffered and rose again on the third day, ascended to the heavens, and will come to judge the living and the dead;
>
> And in the Holy Spirit.
>
> But as for those who say, there was when He was not, and, before being born He was not, and, that He came into existence out of nothing, or who assert that the Son of God is from a different hypostasis or substance, or is created, or is subject to alteration or change—these the Catholic Church anathematizes.[5]

Nicea, coupled with the work done later at the Council of Constantinople in A.D. 381, strongly emphasized the common deity of Father and Son. It also emphasized that the Spirit was fully God proceeding for eternity from the Father through the Son (which Western theologians have understood as the "double procession" of the Spirit). The effect of this theological construction was to preserve an understanding of God that showed him to be fully love within himself. God did not need his creatures to be a loving God. He enjoys in his own family life for eternity a God-centered life of living to love, enjoy, and exalt the other members of the triune family. God is infinitely happy and fulfilled in the delightful communion of Father, Son, and Holy Spirit.

This doctrine of the Trinity brought about an intellectual revolution in the ancient world. The two prevailing worldviews—the Judaistic and the Hellenistic—were now challenged by a third—the trinitarian. An entirely new way to understand ultimate reality (a triune God!) had burst on the scene with the self-disclosure of God in Christ. Nicea was a critical stage in the church's own awareness of this Copernican revolution. A worldview shift of enormous proportions was taking place. The Trinity was reality, and reality never looked so bright and beautiful before.

The Enjoyment of God as Trinity

I have attempted to do what every theologian writing about the Trinity attempts to do—to make comprehensible the incomprehensible mystery of God as Trinity. Yet in fact one doesn't have to understand the "how" of the Trinity's life and nature as long as one can affirm the "that." We do this kind of thing all the time with electronics. I can't explain the technology that lies behind the computer I'm using, but I believe what my manual tells me about motherboards and coprocessors, and I appreciate what it can do. Grace's response to the mystery of the pride of lions speaks of our ability to delight in the truths that exceed our grasp:

> This is still a puzzle to me with all this oneness and threeness going on at the same time. What I am beginning to understand is that the Lion-Lord is like nothing else in the land of Simba; that he is but one Lion-Lord over all things; that he is also and equally a pride of three, Lion-Father, Lionheart and yourself; and that your love is not selfish but is family-centered love. That means that you didn't need to make Africa, or die for us, or make things new again to be loving or overcome loneliness. You were loving within the pride before time began. Your love has always been unselfish and always full.

Grace was right. The doctrine of the Trinity does show us that the love of God has always been unselfish and always full. Consider some of the fullness of this triune love in which we can delight.

The doctrine of the Trinity increases my joy in God as love. God has unbounded joy in the pleasures and perfections of each member of the divine family. The more I think about that and understand that, the more I enjoy God. I enjoy thinking about God's happiness and his gracious desire to share his happiness with us. As John Piper has written, "From all eternity God had beheld the panorama of his own perfections in the face of his Son. All that he is he sees reflected fully and perfectly in the countenance of his Son. And in this he rejoices with infinite joy."[6]

I would add to this only that the Father's love for his Son is not only a love for the "deity" in the Son, but for the special and distinct way the Son mirrors the divine excellencies. For this reason I can say that the Father's loving pleasure in the Son is not just love for himself, but also love for someone who is equal in excellence, but truly other in person. It is other-centered because the Son is truly distinct from the Father. But it is a holy love because it is still God-centered (and not an act of idolatry). I enjoy a God who lives to love, exalt, and live in glad submission to each other in the family and will thrill for eternity that he has brought me into the joys of his family life through Christ.

This appreciation for God's trinitarian love should express itself in my worship. I like Cornelius Plantinga's exhortation that

> our devotion to triune God will include prayer to God the Father (Mt 6:9), through Jesus Christ our Lord (Col 3:17), and in the Spirit (Eph 6:18), always aware that we are invoking not a solitary listener who studies us in splendid isolation, but rather the transcendent family of God. With proper humility and wonder . . .we worship no one person in isolation from the other two. For "the catholic" faith is this: that we worship "one God in Trinity and Trinity in unity" (the Athanasian Creed).[7]

The Trinity focuses my worship and intensifies my joy in such a God.

The doctrine of the Trinity increases my joy in God's work of creation. I have always enjoyed Gerard Manley Hopkins's poem "God's Grandeur":

The world is charged with the grandeur of God.
It will flame out, like shining from shook foil;
It gathers to a greatness, like the ooze of oil
Crushed. Why do men then not reck his rod? . . .

There lives the dearest freshness deep down things;
And through the last lights off the black West went
Oh, morning, at the brown brink eastward, springs—
Because the Holy Ghost over the bent
World broods with warm breast and with ah! bright wings.[8]

What is the grandeur that "flames out, like shining from shook foil"? What is "the dearest freshness deep down things"? It is the love that the triune God has built into everything. Whether I contemplate a landscape or my own "mindscape," whether my eyes drink the morning light that falls off the shiny leaves of the rhododendron outside my study window, or whether they drink the shadows that drape the corners of my psyche—I am witnessing props in the love story of God's family life. Wherever I turn in creation, I see the Father giving fresh gifts to honor, exalt, and celebrate the Son. Wherever I turn in creation, I see the Son giving fresh gifts to his Father. Wherever I turn in creation, I see the "bright wings" of the Spirit bringing forth fresh gifts to express his delight in the Father and the Son.

In other words, the Trinity makes me a lover of the material world. It makes me truly spiritual. I see the goods on the shelf of the store and the leaves on the trees of the woods as spiritual and good because they are the scribbled notes the Trinity sends to one another. Dualism would see certain things in creation and culture as inferior to spiritual things. If you would be truly spiritual then listen to C. S. Lewis's sage advice:

There is no use trying to be more spiritual than God. God never meant man to be a purely spiritual creature. That is why He uses material things like bread and wine to put the new life into us. We may think this rather crude and unspiritual. God invented eating. He likes matter. He invented it.[9]

To know God as Trinity is to know God as loving Creator. Such a knowledge increases my joy in him.

The doctrine of the Trinity increases my awareness and hatred of sin and the Fall. The Trinity helps me to realize what God wants to do with his whole creation, including me: to offer me as a fragrant offering to each of the others in the triune family. In light of this, I look closely at my own life and examine to what degree I honor, exalt and live in glad submission to Father, Son and Spirit. When I do so, I make the same appalling discovery Lewis made about himself. Instead of delight and glad submission I find "a zoo of lusts, a bedlam of ambitions, a nursery of fears, a harem of fondled hatreds. My name [is] legion."[10] I find, in other words, that I am grotesquely out of line with the trinitarian purpose and design for my life. Sin is thus not merely breaking this part of code or that part of custom. Sin is my refusal to delight, honor, and exalt God with my whole life, just as he does himself. Sin is at heart the sacrilege of idolatry—the rejection of trinitarian love and life. Lewis again:

> And indeed the only way in which I can make real to myself what theology teaches about the heinousness of sin is to remember that every sin is the distortion of an energy breathed into us—an energy which, if not thus distorted, would have blossomed into one of those holy acts whereof "God did it" and "I did it" are both true descriptions. We poison the wine as He decants it into us; murder a melody He would play with us as the instrument. We caricature the self-portrait He would paint. Hence all sin, whatever else it is, is sacrilege.[11]

To view ultimate reality as the Trinity and to view creation as the Trinity's expression of its agapic love is to see with growing clarity what's wrong with me and with my world. I have rejected a love that existed before time, murdered a melody that plays in the heart of God. When the truth of Trinity begins to pierce the plated armor of my worldview, I see reality for what it is and my "harem of fondled hatreds" for what they are.

The doctrine of the Trinity increases my joy in God's work of redemption. I must see how an appreciation of the Trinity can renew my joy in God. The long and short of it is this: the Trinity teaches me what God's love is all about and enables me to understand anew that love displayed on the cross. This can best be seen by way of contrast with the other types of love and the coloring they give to redemption.

If God's love is humanistic at heart, then he saves us because he is looking for self-fulfillment in his creation, and his triune identity is largely irrelevant. But if God's love is God-centered (as only the truth of the Trinity establishes), then his love for us is not based on our performance or personal attractiveness or superior qualities but on the existence of family life in God. At great cost and without any achievement on our part, he brings us into his family through the redemption of Christ.

In other words, humanistic concepts of the Trinity tend to reduce it (and God's love in general) to being dependent on humankind. Agapic concepts of the Trinity seek to stress that God, who is the one eternal Creator and Lord of heaven and earth, has complete and full family life and love within himself and needs no one else or nothing else for perfect self-satisfaction and the full experience of love.

Conclusion

God is love because he is Trinity. That has been the refrain of both the parable and the commentary. What did we say about this truth? First, we noted that God is love because he is Trinity, then we insisted on the vital importance of an orthodox understanding of this doctrine, and we concluded that the enjoyment of God as Trinity is central to our Christian life.

I hope the second great conviction that was introduced in the first chapter has been made a bit more understandable and a bit more compelling. Remember what we said on the majesty and Trinity of God?

What is the heart of reality? I am headed in the right direction when I affirm in heart and mind that the triune God is the heart of reality. From the mutual self-giving and joy that each member of the Trinity finds in the other comes the God-centered love that is behind the creation of all things, the judgment of all things, and the redemption of all things.

Questions for Individuals or for Group Discussion

Part One

1. The classic doctrine of the Trinity as stated in the Westminster Confession of Faith is as follows: "In the unity of the Godhead there be three persons, of one substance, power, and eternity—God the Father, God the Son, and God the Holy Ghost. The Father is of none, neither begotten nor proceeding; the Son is eternally begotten of the Father; the Holy Ghost, eternally proceeding from the Father and the Son." Are each of these points affirmed in the parable? Explain.

2. Mumo's theology of self-centeredness actually came from his view of Simba as the one creator of Africa. Can a bare monotheism encourage

selfishness and self-centeredness? Explain.

3. When the children were shown the four statues, Simba said, "There are not four lions. There are three lions and one Lion-Lord. The three lions are the one Lion-Lord." Is this an adequate description of the Trinity? Give reasons for your answer.

4. Simba said that "we live to love, exalt, and enjoy the other members of the pride, and everything we do and say is for the good pleasure of the other." What biblical evidence shows that this is true of the Trinity?

5. The doctrine of the Trinity has always been threatened by tritheism (where the threeness is stressed to the sundering of the one divine essence) on the one side and bare monotheism on the other (where the one essence is stressed to the neglect of the threeness). Imagine a continuum with monotheism at one end and tritheism at the other. Where on this continuum do you think this parable comes down?

6. Grace's final words in the parable are her attempt to identify the Trinity's motive behind creation and redemption: "Your love is not self-love but is family-centered love. . . . Your love has always been unselfish and always full." How does the doctrine of the Trinity protect God from being charged with a self-centered love? Or is it permissible for God to be self-centered? Explain.

7. What insights have you gained from the parable about the family life of God that might increase your love and joy in God? Give reasons for your answers.

Part Two

8. What do you think of the statement that "God is love because he is Trinity"?

What ideas in the "theology behind the story" section support that statement?

9. What evidence from the Gospels do you find the most revealing of the "love life" of God?

10. What was wrong with Arius's understanding of God?

How did the Nicene Creed deal with his errors?

11. What are some of the ways the Trinity can increase our joy in God?

Which of the ideas is most helpful to you at this point in your thinking? Why?

For Further Reading

Royce Gruenler, *The Trinity in the Gospel of John* (Grand Rapids: Baker, 1986), shows that the doctrine of the Trinity is not based on a few proof texts but is central to the entire Fourth Gospel. It also shows how a lively emphasis on the Trinity can overcome some of the modern distortions of God, such as those found in process theology. Peter Toon and James Spiceland, eds., *One God in Trinity* (Westchester, Ill: Cornerstone, 1980), is a very fine collection of essays by evangelical theologians on the centrality of the Trinity to our faith. J. N. D. Kelly, *Early Christian Doctrine* (New York: Harper & Row, 1959), is a good source for understanding the historical battles that helped shaped the orthodox doctrine of the Trinity.

Chapter Four
The Attributes of God:
Harlowe's Biggest
Case

Harlowe *looked out the* window of his smoky second-floor office overlooking a grimy Los Angeles street. Curls of smoke from his cigarette waved in front of his eyes, but not enough to deflect his gaze from the woman in red making a straight line for his office.

Within two minutes there was a knock at the door. "It's open," Harlowe mumbled with his usual prep-school charm.

A woman enveloped in a cloud of perfume and decked out in red from heels to hat strode in. "Pleased to meet you, Miss Riding Hood," Harlowe said, staring into her wide and heavily made-up eyes. "I can be either grandma or the big bad wolf for the right price. Fifty bucks a day plus expenses."

"Mr. Harlowe," the woman said, ignoring his comments, "I'm Vivian Spencer, and I want you to solve the strangest case ever offered to you."

Strangest case? Harlowe whistled through his teeth, sizing up this goddess-like creature while mentally riffling through the house of horrors that made up his career as a private investigator. Perverts, geeks, nerds, hookers, bikers, psychos, slashers, pushers, rapists, sadists . . . his file was full of such cases. He'd even had a few strange cases now and again. Harlowe flicked some ash from his cigarette toward one of the less filthy chairs in his office. Vivian sat down. Harlowe just stared.

"I want you to locate some missing articles," Vivian said hesitantly. "I know they're out there . . . but they have been . . . shall we say, misplaced."

"For fifty a day plus expenses we shall say misplaced," Harlowe said as he continued sizing up this uptown dame carefully. "Just what are these 'missing articles'?"

"Attributes of God," said Vivian with great seriousness. "You know, omniscience, omnipotence, eternity, impassibility, omnipresence . . ."

"I've heard of them," Harlowe said brusquely, afraid she might dump the whole Westminster Catechism's definition of God on him. "What's your angle?"

"Worship, Mr. Harlowe," the woman in red said with rising feeling. "How can I worship God without these attributes? Every service I go to now has a God who is user-friendly, who does nice things to nice people, is one with the earth, is a cosmic puppy dog, a projection of our exalted selves . . ."

"Any suspects?" Harlowe asked coolly, blowing smoke at the bare bulb dangling from the cracked plaster ceiling.

"I think process theology and secular humanism have stripped God of these transcendent attributes, and I'm having trouble even praying now. Harlowe, you must help me find a church that still teaches God's majestic attributes," Vivian said, sobbing and dabbing her eyes with a lace-lined white Irish linen handkerchief with pink roses embroidered on the border.

"Excuse me," said Harlowe, "but aren't those pink roses embroidered on the border of your Irish linen handkerchief?"

"Oh, what does it matter anymore?" she sobbed, burying her head in her hands. Harlowe was going to press her on the pink roses but decided to back off.

"That'll do," said Harlowe. "I'll take the case."

Vivian stood up, sniffed, smoothed her dress, and walked out the door. On the table next to her chair she had dropped her card. "29 Hillcrest Drive" was embossed on the shiny surface of the card. Harlowe picked it up, grabbed his hat and coat, slipped his gun into its holster, and headed off to Fat Eddie's.

"Fat Eddie's out back," the bartender told Harlowe after the PI had rearranged part of the smaller man's face. Harlowe walked the length of the pool hall and pulled open the far door, gun in hand. Fat Eddie was crouched over a pool cue eyeing a big-money shot against Lean Lenny Repulso, who was standing in the heavily shadowed corner.

"Pleasure to see you, Harlowe," Eddie said, wiping the sweat from several layers of fat that dangled under his chin. "You know Lenny."

"If I wanted chitchat, I'd join a bridge club," Harlowe said, thinking how much trouble he had suppressing that boyhood charm that just oozed out so naturally. "I'm looking for some missing attributes, belonging to you-know-who."

Lenny and Fat Eddie shot meaningful glances at each other.

Harlowe continued. "I couldn't help but notice those meaningful glances that you shot at each other. And while you're spilling your guts, tell me everything you know about pink embroidered roses."

Fat Eddie and Lean Lenny each stood motionless, looking at him without any expression. "Forty-first and Vine," said Fat Eddie finally, wiping the sweat off his face. "But don't tell the process theology people I told you."

Harlowe got to the corner of Forty-first and Vine in about twenty minutes. He looked up and saw a large Gothic-style cathedral. The sign in front read, "The Church of the Holy Attributes." As Harlowe got out of his car, he almost stumbled over a body lying on the sidewalk in front of him. It was a wino who seemed to be alive, though not kicking. Harlowe pulled the man to his feet, dragged him down to the corner and into a coffee shop, and propped him up in a booth. He then slipped five bucks to a waitress and told her to pump the man with coffee and sandwiches. He'd be back.

Harlowe made his way to the front entrance of the cathedral. He could see a tour group walking through and stopping for a few minutes in front of each of the attributes of God displayed in the lavish stained-glass windows that lined the upper portions of the church nave. He joined the group and listened in on the description of the attributes provided by the elderly guide, who spoke in a thick Irish accent:

"Mind the four main windows that dominate the four walls of the cathedral," said the guide, casting a sideways glance at Harlowe as he slipped to the edge of the small crowd. "They each stand for one of four major groupings of God's attributes: the glory of God, the holiness of God, the lordship of God, and the love of God."

Harlowe looked around at the four main windows, and sure enough, they were all labeled just as the guide had said. This man was a real oracle, Harlowe thought. The guide continued to drone on. "This first window is dedicated to the cluster of attributes that are summarized as the glory of God. They are symbolized by the Trinity circled by a blazing light in the north window. In this cluster are the perfections of transcendence, which include the attributes of infinity, self-existence, and immutability. There are those that have attacked this window before. Seem to hate the notion that God might be the center of the universe instead of themselves."

Harlowe was getting a little restless with all this transcendent God-talk. Scanning the expanse of the cathedral floor area, he spotted a figure in dark clothing slipping from shadow to shadow.

Harlowe yawned as the guide moved on.

"The next window, with the picture of three roses on a common stem, has as its theme the holiness of the Trinity, with its cluster of attributes including righteousness, justice, wrath, and goodness."

Harlowe was getting more restless as the guide continued his explanations. But a distraction rescued him. The wino whom he had left at the restaurant had staggered in. He was heading toward the last window. The dark figure who seemed to be trying to hide could not be seen now, but was somewhere over in that same corner. Staying with the group enabled Harlowe to keep his eye on the unfolding drama by the last window without being conspicuous. The voice of the Irishman broke Harlowe's train of thought.

"Window three is on the lordship of God and deals with the attributes of omnipotence, omnipresence, and omniscience, which are represented by the Trinity holding the earth and the stars in their hands." The group was moving toward the fourth window now. This final window was the most intriguing, for it had the triangular symbol that denoted the Trinity, but in front of the Trinity was the figure of a fool, a court jester complete with funny face and jester's cap. A biblical reference, 1 Corinthians 1:25, was inscribed just below the frame of the window. Harlowe could now see that the wino was kneeling down before the fool and praying, soft sobs rising from his bent form.

The guide spoke again. "This final window deals with the love of God and concerns his mercy, jealousy and grace. And according to the artist who designed it, it also deals with two attributes of God that are rarely discussed—his foolishness and weakness."

As the guide spoke those words, the dark figure jumped from the shadows and hurled what appeared to be a brick at the figure of the fool. The brick's impact shattered the yellow and red glass into a thousand shards, which exploded upon the heads of the tourists below.

Harlowe sprang after the dark figure. He grabbed at a white object in the vandal's hand. In the next moment Harlowe was down, sprawling on the stone floor amid the broken glass. The toothless and apologetic grin of the wino, whom he had stumbled over once again, greeted him. Harlowe got up and brushed himself off, realizing that the hoodlum had escaped. He leaned over and picked something off the floor. It was a white linen handkerchief with pink roses embroidered on the border.

Harlowe arrived at 29 Hillcrest Drive about forty minutes after the incident in the cathedral, making just one quick stop at a toy store on the way. He was ushered into the sitting room, and in a few minutes, Vivian Spencer, in a satin dressing gown, was offering him a drink.

Harlowe declined. "Just came by to say I'm off the case and to return two items that I think you might need."

Vivian was visibly tense but asked in as casual a tone as she could, "And what two items might they be, Mr. Harlowe?"

"One is your handkerchief, which you dropped in the cathedral after you put a brick through the fourth window. I think I know why you did it. The other item is a gift from me. Think of it every time you go to church. And let me leave you with a tip: You need all four windows to worship."

Harlowe stood up, shot a sideways glance at an elegantly wrapped box he had placed on the table beside his chair, and without saying goodby, showed himself out.

Vivian listened as the roar of his car faded down the driveway. She walked over to the box, tore it open, and gasped. Inside, wearing a clownlike grin, was a stuffed doll resembling the fool in the cathedral window. Her linen handkerchief had been placed in the doll's cloth hand. Vivian took the handkerchief and opened it out. She saw the familiar lace and the roses embroidered on the edge. A new decoration had been added, however. Written across the center of the handkerchief was a reference to a Bible passage. Vivian sat in rage while her knuckles became as white as the Irish linen handkerchief clutched in her fists.

The Theology Behind the Story: **The Attributes of God**

"Worship, Mr. Harlowe," the woman in red said with rising feeling. "How can I worship God without these attributes? Every service I go to now has a God who is user-friendly, who does nice things to nice people, is one with the earth, is a cosmic puppy dog, a projection of our exalted selves . . ."

With these words, Vivian reminds us how central a study of God's attributes is to knowing and enjoying him. Seeing God as Trinity and living with an awareness of his mutual love within the divine family is the most important part of theology. But we must build on our trinitarian understanding of our God by exploring his attributes.

Learning to worship God as Trinity, I am suggesting, involves more than just searching for creative techniques. We need to know about the nature of our triune God if we are to worship and enjoy him properly. The objective for us in this chapter is to increase our worship by sensing what an immense treasure God is. Insights are more important than incense and truth more vital than technique when it comes to fueling the furnace of worship and generating the heat of glad submission.

The Existence and Attributes of God Are Under Attack

Orthodoxy has long talked about God in terms of his attributes or perfections. Such attributes have often been divided into groups of *communicable* attributes (those that can be reflected in his creatures, like goodness and mercy) and *incommunicable* attributes (those that can't be copied or reflected by the creature, such as omnipresence or omniscience). Orthodoxy was fond of saying, with strong biblical support, that God not only has attributes but *is* his attributes—they are perfections of his nature and character. This concept of God has dominated Christian worship for centuries. But voices of dissent have now been raised.

In the parable, Vivian was exaggerating when she complained that she could not find a church where God's majesty and transcendence were taken seriously. But she was correct that the critics of God's majesty are beginning to create some disturbing static. When Harlowe asked whether she had any suspects who might be responsible for the demise of a majestic view of God, Vivian named a couple: "I think process theology and secular humanism have stripped God of these transcendent attributes, and I'm having trouble even praying now." She then added plaintively, "Harlowe, you must help me find a church that still teaches God's majestic attributes."

The attack on the God of the Bible (or classic theism) has been sharp and sustained. Process theology is one attempt to revise Christian theism to make it more compatible with modern scientific and intellectual trends. Process theology begins with the assumption that reality is the process of becoming and not a static state of being. For God to be real, says the process theologian, God must be changing and growing—not the static God of orthodoxy. God is "dipolar" for the process theologian. God has a side of his being that is beyond the universe but also has a side that is identical with the universe. The universe is God's body. Human minds are God's brain cells. God is, then, dependent on and identical to the universe and yet, in some mysterious way, beyond the universe and independent of it. This is not *pantheism* (God equals the creation) but rather *panentheism* (God is in but not limited to everything in creation).

Neoclassical theism, though rejecting process theology, is similarly critical of orthodox theism and the traditional understanding of God's attributes. Clark Pinnock is an example of an evangelical theologian who has been vocal in his rejection of God's unchangeableness, timelessness, and impassibility. Pinnock asserts that Greek logic, not divine revelation, is the source of such attributes of God.[1] Though much closer to classical theism than to process theology, neoclassical theism argues that the traditional picture of God presents a cold and uncaring deity who is difficult to like or love.

In contrast to these calls for major revisions in the portrait of God drawn by orthodox Christianity, I would like to suggest that the historic view may well be the best and most biblical description of God available. Perhaps the best summary of this classic view of God is found in the answer to the question "What is God?" in the Westminster Shorter Catechism: "God is a Spirit, infinite, eternal, and unchangeable, in his being, wisdom, power, justice, goodness, and truth."[2] But before we open up this classic understanding of God's attributes, we must look at two attributes that may help to blunt some of the criticisms leveled at the orthodox picture of God. These are God's attributes of weakness and folly.

The Love of the Triune God Is Best Revealed in the Weakness and Folly of the Cross

Standard treatments of the love of God mention his mercy, grace and jealousy (some include his goodness under this heading). I emphasized in the last chapter that God's love must be understood in a radically God-centered way—as the Father, Son, and Spirit living to honor, exalt, and enjoy one another eternally. God is love because he is Trinity. But this God-centered love overflows to his creatures, and the rich and swift currents and eddies of God's love can be summed up by those three attributes. His mercy is his compassionate love for sinners who do not deserve the redemption in Christ that he offers. His grace likewise speaks of his free favor granted to sinners. God's jealousy reminds us that he loves us with a covenant love that is like the covenant of marriage, and thus binds all parties to faithfulness. As James Garrett explains, the "jealousy of God is . . . the intensity of his holiness in demanding and expecting the ready and undivided allegiance of his human creatures, especially those in covenant with him."[3]

Yet more is said in the parable about God's love beside these more familiar attributes. The strangest part of the parable, for many readers, at least, is the scene before the fourth window of the cathedral. Recall the description of the window:

> The group was moving toward the fourth window now. This final window was the most intriguing, for it had the triangular symbol that denoted the Trinity, but in front of the Trinity was the figure of a fool, a court jester complete with funny face and jester's cap. A biblical reference, 1 Corinthians 1:25, was inscribed just below the frame of the window. Harlowe could now see that the wino was kneeling down before the fool and praying, soft sobs rising from his bent form.

The picture in this fourth window seems almost blasphemous. How can our almighty God ever be called weak and foolish by those who claim that they seek to glorify him by enjoying him?

Consider the words of 1 Corinthians 1:25: "For the foolishness of God is wiser than man's wisdom, and the weakness of God is stronger than man's strength." This passage explicitly refers to these two "attributes." But what did Paul mean by the foolishness and weakness of God? Let's be clear that God is neither foolish nor weak. God is all-wise and all-powerful. Why then this kind of language? Martin Luther has helped to answer this question for me.

Luther did more than protest indulgences and call for a return to justification by faith. Luther also rejected the traditional way of discussing God by his transcendent attributes (like omniscience and omnipotence), calling it a "theology of glory" that talks of God in glowing terms but at the same time fills humanity with the pride of knowledge and the spirit of self-righteousness. Such a theology may be technically correct and orthodox, but it is damning, for its seeks God outside the cross, the only authorized place where he is revealed and is to be found. Thus "Luther feels that since man's fall into sin, true theology is possible only as a theology of the cross."[4] Without recognizing our state of fallenness and approaching God directly to see him in his attributes, we will surely misuse that information.

Does such an approach to God, understanding him first in his compassion and mercy before we move on to his transcendence and majesty, render God's infinite attributes irrelevant and unworthy of the Christian's attention? Quite the contrary, for the cross unlocks the significance of God's power and amplifies the fullness of his majesty. How? Consider the explanation of Paul Althaus:

> God shows that he is God precisely in the fact that he is mighty in weakness, glorious in lowliness, living and life-giving in death. Thus in Luther's thinking the theology of the cross and God's being God are most intimately connected.[5]

Thus we must reject natural theology and theistic proofs and all such attempts to approach God outside of the cross. In the final analysis, we must not trust reason or experience to know God. God will be a puzzle and problem to us if we seek to know him from circumstances or syllogisms alone. God is revealed best where he is hidden most—in the dark shadows of weakness and defeat that surround his death on the cross. He is glorious in his weakness. He is majestic in his folly. He is transcendent in his death on the cross. He is a God who brings things out of their opposites.

As we think of God, then we must make the cross central. We must approach God and his attributes through Good Friday first. When we do that, our understanding of the fullness of who he is breaks out with a joy like that of Easter morning.

The Triune God Is Glorious and Transcendent

Harlowe's cathedral tour began where one might expect to begin when discussing God's attributes—namely, with his glory and transcendence. The guide told the people gathered around him that to speak of God's glory and transcendence is to speak of a cluster of attributes. It also means speaking about the whole Trinity. In light of the cross of Christ we understand God's transcendence in a different way than the devout Muslim or Jew would understand this concept, but we still cling powerfully to this attribute as essential in understanding God. Let's take a look at what this cluster means.

God is glorious and transcendent. God's glory fills the pages of Scripture, from the drama of Sinai (Ex 19-24) to the visions of Revelation (Rev 1:14-16). God's glory shines in the face of Christ (2 Cor 4:6). The meaning of this attribute is roughly that God's surpassing greatness and majesty silence all human pretensions to greatness and glory. God is incomparable. Here's where the answer to question 4 of the Westminster Shorter Catechism belongs: "God is a Spirit, infinite, eternal, and unchangeable, in his being, wisdom, power, justice, goodness, and truth."[6] To say that God is transcendent and glorious is to say that he is the one and only infinite and unchangeable Spirit in all of reality (Jn 4:24). Because we believe in the glory of God, we affirm with the Scriptures that he has certain incommunicable attributes that make up his glory and surpassing greatness as an infinite Spirit. These would include his infinity, immutability, and impassibility.

God is infinite. God is without limits. Isaiah 40 describes the nations of the earth as but a "drop in the bucket" compared with God, for although they possess power and majesty and greatness, there are limits to each of those attributes when applied to a nation. There are no limits to those attributes when they are applied to God. Nonsense limits ("Can God make a rock too big for himself to lift?" or "Can God make a square triangle?") are really descriptions of "no-things" and are, therefore, not true limits that would qualify God's infinity.

God is self-existent. Acts 17:25 tells us that God needs nothing but everything needs God. He depends on nothing else or no one else for life, but all things and everyone depend on him for life, for "he himself gives all men life and breath and everything else." We sometimes use the term *aseity* to describe this attribute of God, thus referring to his absolute self-existence and independence from his creation.

God is immutable. God's being is pure infinite activity. God has no undeveloped potential and is thus "full grown" and not under development as in process theology and neoclassical theism. "I the Lord do not change"(Mal 3:6).

God is impassible. God does not suffer as human beings suffer. He is not surprised by grief as we are, nor can he be victimized as we are. Most treatments of impassibility wrestle with the understanding of the church fathers that God has no capacity to suffer, meaning that the world's events do not inflict pain in God, for God is infinitely separated from the world and cannot be made its victim. Yet that does not square with God's pain in watching his Son die on the cross or watching his people worship idols.

I want to deal with this in more depth in our discussion of providence ("Huck and Jim Meet Their Author"), but at this point I simply point out that whatever pain God feels must be eternal and unchanging pain, for otherwise his attribute of suffering would be dependent on humanity. Impassibility protects God's internal suffering from being understood either as merely a copy of human pain or as pain inflicted upon him by his creation.

Such is the greatness of the God who has disclosed himself to us in Christ. So far surpassing humankind in every way but sin, such a God deserves the epithet of "wholly other." As Bruce Milne says, "This view of God is anathema to modern man," for they want a small god easily manipulated.[7] The bankruptcy of liberalism with its God who is too small becomes apparent in light of the biblical witness to God's infinite majesty. That majesty leads us to recognize the triune God as an all-powerful Lord.

The Triune God Is All-Powerful

Harlowe's cathedral tour brought him to a third window where God's power was portrayed:

> The droning voice of the Irishman broke Harlowe's train of thought. "Window three is on the lordship of God and deals with the attributes of omnipotence, omnipresence, and omniscience, which are represented by the Trinity holding the earth and the stars in their hands."

Let's examine these three words to see what they reveal to us about our triune God.

God is omnipotent. When God gave his covenant name, Yahweh, to Moses he was asserting that all power belonged to him. "I am what I am" or "I will be what I will be" speaks of God's self-determining power. Nothing or no one else, not even powerful Pharaoh, can thwart the self-determining one. When the Bible asks, "Is anything to hard for the Lord?" (Gen 18:14), the consistent answer is "no." He gives sons to barren wombs, saviors through virgin births, victory through defeat, regeneration to stony hearts, and all manner of other impossible accomplishments. He sets the rise and fall of nations (Acts 17:26) as well as the life span of sparrows (Mt 10:29). He never tires, hungers, or sleeps. He is a God of inexhaustible energy and power.

God is omnipresent. Psalm 139 records the writer's marvel that God's Spirit cannot be eluded. God is omnipresent in all of time and space. God sees all things because his searching presence is everywhere. Though initially a terrifying truth to the psalmist, who appears at first to want to escape from God, God's omnipresence becomes a deep comfort to the writer when he finally puts himself in God's strong arms and realizes that he can never be truly alone again.

God is omniscient. God knows all things. This is linked to his omnipresence in Psalm 139:1-4:

> O LORD, you have searched me and you know me. You know when I sit and when I rise; you perceive my thoughts from afar. You discern my going out and my lying down; you are familiar with all my ways.
>
> Before a word is on my tongue you know it completely, O LORD.

Compare this powerful proclamation with the equally dramatic claims of Hebrews 4:13: "Nothing in all creation is hidden from God's sight. Everything is uncovered and laid bare before the eyes of him to whom we must give account."

Our triune God holds the stars and earth in his hands. He is omnipotent, omnipresent, and omniscient. In light of the cross and the fact that this kind of God is now for me in Christ and not against me, his all-powerful lordship is a truth to treasure greatly.

The Triune God Is Holy

The cathedral guide brought the tour before a window with roses:

> The next window, with the picture of three roses on a common stem, has as its theme the holiness of the Trinity, with its cluster of attributes including righteousness, justice, wrath, and goodness.

Why roses? The beauty of God's holiness is the principal reason for the image. God's holiness is linked with the Hebrew word *quodesh,* which has as its fundamental meaning "separation." Two ideas are paramount in this attribute. First, God's holiness means that God is unique. There is no one or nothing like him (cf. Is 6:1-4; 57:15; 1 Sam 2:2). He is in a class by himself as Creator and sovereign and should receive the recognition and worship that his unique status deserves.

Second, God's holiness is also an ethical reality. God is morally pure.

Habakkuk says to God (in 1:13), "Your eyes are too pure to look on evil; you cannot tolerate wrong." Because God is triune, the essence of God's holiness is in the infinite love and devotion that Father, Son, and Spirit enjoy with one another. God is God-centered without measure. Because God is weak and foolish enough to save sinners on the cross, we must also see the Trinity's holiness in terms of holy love redeeming sinners in a way that perfectly meets the demands of moral purity.

Brief comments on these beauties of God may help us enjoy the aroma of these roses more fully.

First, the righteousness of God must be noted. This refers to the fact that God acts in accordance with his character: he does what is right because he is radically God-centered. The Bible is full of references to God's righteousness (Ps 31:1; Jer 11:20). The righteousness of God has now been shared with us in Christ who makes us pleasing to a righteous God through the death of Christ (Rom 1:17; 3:21ff.).[8]

Second, the justice of God is crucial to understanding his holiness. The justice of God refers to God's power to do what is fair and to judge impartially (Rom 2:8, 11). God's fairness may seem rather uneven in the distribution of wealth and opportunity around the contemporary world, but he will bring all things to perfect justice in his time and in his way. "The last will be first and the first will be last" (Mt 20:16).

Third, the wrath of God is a necessary aspect of God's holiness. This refers to God's holy hatred of sin and evil (Rom 1:18ff.). John Murray called it "the holy revulsion of God's being against that which is the contradiction of his holiness."[9] Like all of his other attributes, God's wrath flows from his love, for the presence of deep love necessitates the hatred of that which threatens or opposes what is loved. The love of life necessitates the hatred of death. The love of fidelity necessitates the hatred of infidelity. So the Trinity's infinite love for one another necessitates a wrath and hatred against anything that would dishonor, diminish, or decline to enjoy the persons of the divine family. This wrath of God was poured out upon the head of Christ for us (Rom 3:25; Eph 2:3; Jn 3:36). Luther called this attribute of God his "strange work" because his "proper work," which we discover when we look at God through the cross, is salvation.

Fourth, the holiness of God includes the goodness of God. God's goodness consists primarily in the service and disposability of each member of the Trinity to the other and in creation (Ps 100:5; 145:8-9; Lam 3:25; Mt 7:11; Acts 14:17; Jas 1:5, 17). God would be infinitely and eternally good even if there had been no creation in which to display that goodness. Some theologians place all of God's moral attributes under goodness.[10] God's care for his people and his sovereign preservation of all things are rich displays of this perfection of goodness. The cross is the supreme display of his goodness, for there the loving service of the Son to the Father in redeeming a fallen world revealed the infinite heart of goodness in God.

Such is God's perfection of holiness. A rose may not be the best picture of the holiness of God with its righteousness, justice, wrath, and goodness, but it does remind us of one thing: his holiness is a thing of beauty, and when its aroma fills the days of our lives, his beauty begins to fill us with delight and joy in him.

The Triune God Is Worthy of Worship

The parable ends with Harlowe offering some spiritual counsel to his complicated client, Vivian: "You need all four windows to worship." Harlowe's solution to Vivian's problem at the beginning of the story (a God she can worship) is thus summarized. To approach God outside the cross is to face a distorted image. To approach God through the cross but blind to his attributes is to devalue our redemption and the majesty of a God who is strong enough to bring life out of death and victory out of defeat. We need all four windows to worship.

But what exactly is this much-commanded response to a God of such majesty and beauty? What exactly is worship, and how can it be intensified by these truths?

Worship can be defined as delighting in God. Christ's powerful statement of worship in the Gospel of John pushes us in the direction of such a definition:

> Yet a time is coming and has now come when the true worshipers will worship the Father in spirit and truth, for they are the kind of worshipers the Father seeks. God is spirit, and his worshipers must worship in spirit and in truth. (Jn 4:23-24)

Christ intends to make a worshiper of God out of this prodigal daughter from Samaria. Analyze the verse, and the components of true worship fall out of it like ripe fruit from a tree:

> The fuel of worship is the truth of God, the furnace of worship is the spirit of man, and the heat of worship is the vital affections of reverence, contrition, trust, gratitude and joy. . . . There must [also] be ignition and fire. This is the Holy Spirit.[11]

I will offer a definition of worship in light of the above thoughts: *Worship is that act of the Holy Spirit in the believer which produces expressions of deep delight in God flowing from a heart and mind stirred by biblical truth about God and his beauty.*

Luther's reminder about the theology of the cross becomes crucial for this kind of true worship. I can approach God with desire and longing for him only through the cross, and not outside it. God's naked attributes would cause me terror and not delight were it not for the vanquishing of sin, wrath, Satan and the grave in the death of Christ. Only the cross enables me to have "empty hands," to get my mind off self-justification long enough to adore a God who became weak in his omnipotence so that I might enjoy the rich delights of his person.

But doesn't this emphasis on worship as enjoying God or experiencing him as our greatest treasure actually place too much emphasis on pleasure and not enough on obedience and duty? I like John Piper's answer:

> The enemy of worship is not that our desire for pleasure is too strong but too weak! We have settled for a home, a family, a few friends, a job, a television, a microwave oven, an occasional night out, a yearly vacation, and perhaps a new personal computer. We have accustomed ourselves to such meager, short-lived pleasures that our capacity for joy has shriveled. And so our worship has shriveled.[12]

If delight is a necessary part of worship, and worship is a constant part of our Christian life, then should we not always be full of joy? Shouldn't we always be overflowing with the vital affections of love and adoration? If that seems unrealistic, we need to be reminded that there is a cycle to worship that should not be forgotten. True worship of God involves moving through three emotional stages.

Various stages of worship are found in Psalm 73, stages that Asaph followed from the unresponsive and bitter stage reflected in verses 21 and 22 ("I was senseless and ignorant; I was a brute beast before you") to the stage of joy and satisfaction in God ("earth has nothing I desire besides you," v. 25).

According to Piper's analysis, delighting in God begins with the *stage of barrenness,* where every drop of joy and gladness has vanished and our souls are parched and discouraged. The second stage of worship is the *stage of longing,* where we hunger and thirst for God, although our hearts are still unsatisfied (Ps 42:1-2). If we patiently and prayerfully persevere in our intention to be satisfied in God through these lower stages of worship, God in his grace will give us the fruit of full satisfaction in him (Ps 73:25). Thus the third and final stage of worship is the *stage of satisfaction.*

This cycle of worship undoubtedly has daily patterns as well as long-term patterns. The point is that worship is a fruit of the Spirit and that the process of fruit-bearing requires these various stages. Every aspect of our emotional life, every mood, can be fertilizer for the cultivation of true worship. We are always in a position to worship God, whether through barrenness (glorifying him by my need), longing (glorifying him through my desire for him), or satisfaction (glorifying him through expressions of joy and gladness that overflow a satisfied heart).

But whatever our mood or state of mind, this truth remains—God is worthy to be worshiped.

Conclusion

How can I worship God? That's what Vivian's problem was. She had some serious hang-ups, however. She was willing to marvel at his majesty but couldn't get past his folly on the cross. Her worship of God ultimately ended in rejection of God. She needed "to get her mind right" before progress in worship could be possible. Therefore, as we have seen, insights, not incense, are the key; truth, not techniques, are most critical. What truths can fuel the furnace of worship? We examined six affirmations inspired by the parable that could make a difference in worshiping our triune God in consecrated lifestyles as well as in corporate liturgies. This renewed worship flows from a new awareness that, first, the existence and attributes of God are under attack; second, the love of the triune God is best revealed through the weakness and folly of the cross; third, the triune God is glorious and transcendent; fourth, the triune God is all-powerful; fifth, the triune God is holy; and finally, the triune God is worthy of worship.

Some might say at this point that these attributes are a little abstract and nebulous. How can we make them more concrete? No need to worry. God has done just that. He has displayed the fullness of his glory in his works of creation, providence, judgment, and redemption. We turn in the next chapter to the display of his greatness and goodness in the act of creation.

Questions for Individuals or Group Discussion

Part One

1. What is the primary use of the attributes mentioned in the parable?
   What are some other reasons we need to know about God's perfection?
2. What are the attributes of God's glory mentioned by the guide?
   What key texts describe these attributes?
   How would you define each of the attributes in this cluster?
3. What are the attributes of God's lordship? Find biblical support for this cluster, and give a succinct definition of each including what these attributes tell us about the Trinity and our proper response to the Trinity.
4. Is the window with the three roses on a common stem a proper symbol for God's holiness? Give support for your response.
   Look at each of the attributes in this cluster. What role do these perfections play in understanding creation, fall, and redemption?
5. Why did Vivian Spencer want to destroy the fourth window?
   Why did she scrunch up her handkerchief in rage?
6. What role does the wino play in the story?
   In what ways does he shed light on the nature of true worship?
   How does one become a "wino" in worship?
7. Why did Harlowe give Vivian the doll and say to her: "You need all four windows to worship"? Do you agree or disagree? Why?

Part Two

8. Is it appropriate to talk of God's weakness and folly as attributes? Explain.
   What are the benefits of looking at God in light of the cross?

Was this perspective of the cross kept consistently as the other perfections of God were discussed, or did a theology of glory emerge to eclipse the theology of the cross? Explain.

9. What are the arguments for and against applying the attribute of impassibility to God?

What scriptural evidence might be marshaled for either position?

Where do you come down on the question?

10. How important is God's wrath in completing the picture of God's holiness?

What does this say about the issue of God's impassibility?

11. Consider the Westminster Shorter Catechism's description of God: "God is a Spirit, infinite, eternal, and unchangeable, in his being, wisdom, power, holiness, justice, goodness, and truth" (question 4). What are the strengths of this definition?

Are there any glaring omissions?

In what ways do the parable and the "Theology Behind the Story" section support such an understanding of God? In what ways, if any, do they differ?

12. Evaluate the definition of worship given in this chapter. How would you improve upon it?

13. Are these three stages of worship valid?

What comfort could understanding stages of worship be to a struggling Christian who doesn't always "feel like" worshiping on a Sunday morning?

14. How might believers use the truth about God's majesty and perfections to fuel their joy and delight in him?

How would you use this information in your personal worship?

How would you design a corporate worship experience to communicate the truths about God's majesty developed in this chapter?

For Further Reading

Alister McGrath's *Meaning of the Cross* (Grand Rapids: Zondervan, 1988) explores Luther's theology of the cross and its importance in understanding God. His more recent book *Roots That Refresh: A Celebration of Reformation Spirituality* (London: Hodder and Stoughton, 1992) is a penetrating look at how the theology of the cross transforms our understanding of God, personal worship, and holiness. John Piper's *Desiring God* (Portland: Multnomah Press, 1984) discusses worship as an aspect of Christian hedonism. Stephen Charnock's *Existence and Attributes of God* (Grand Rapids: Baker, 1979, reprint) is a time-honored treatment of God's majesty. Although it was originally published in the seventeenth century, it has been reprinted in various editions in our own century. Finally, I cannot fail to mention J. I. Packer's spiritual classic, *Knowing God* (Downers Grove, Ill.: IVP, 1973).

Chapter Five
Creation: The Last Adventure of Ebenezer Scrooge

Old *Ebenezer Scrooge was dead*. Not stuffed in a pine box and buried under six feet of frozen turf—no, not dead like that. But the old Scrooge—the cold-hearted Scrooge who hated life, children, and Christmas—was dead and gone. The new Scrooge, looking out from his flat over the gas-lit London streets below, was a changed man now, full of joy and good will. The impact of the three spirits who had visited him several Christmases ago was lasting. Scrooge had vowed that he would be different, and he was as good as his word.

New Ebenezer Scrooge was tired. Not tired of Christmas and its message of Christ, but tired with a strange weariness that had settled on his heart. That afternoon on his way home from the orphanage where he had handed out countless gifts to needy children, he had felt the weight of his weariness. He had wandered past the brightly lit bookshops on Charing Cross and felt empty of his normal passion to browse. He walked past the glittering toy shops of Piccadilly Circus and felt no gladness at the painted puppets or the shining trains that filled the frosted windows. He passed the butcher's shop in Covent Gardens and took no pleasure in the plump geese that hung from the butcher's hooks. Even watching children making angels in the new snow depressed him. The bodies sinking into the snow reminded him of corpses being lowered into graves.

Scrooge knew that the problem wasn't with his view of Christmas but with his view of creation. He realized that he needed to restore his enthusiasm for life in general—the good creation around him of land and people and painted puppets—if he wanted his satisfaction in Christmas to return. Perhaps part of his weariness was the frustration of knowing that there was more joy to draw from the richness of life in general, and Christmas in particular, than he seemed able to experience. From his previous experiences Scrooge knew that the greatest loss in life is the loss of the capacity to enjoy life.

As Scrooge sat by his window thinking about these things, he raised toward the reading lamp the old leather book that had been resting in his lap. It was a book of memorabilia about the Scrooge family. Scrooge opened to the first page and glanced at the poem he had read aloud a hundred times in the last few weeks. The poem was entitled "The Song of Creation" and was an anonymous poem about the origin of the Scrooge clan. Scrooge had turned to this poem to see whether it might help him restore his joy in the sights and smells of good books and plump geese. Scrooge read the words aloud again:

Your pen scribbled long with joy and glory,
And then wrote the words that made our story;
In a matter of days you framed each plot,
From Oliver's twists to Copperfield's lot;
From the Scrooges high to the Cratchetts low,
You shaped each creature from head to toe;
Your chapters were good from end to start,
And told us much of your Family heart;
And when all was done you rested well,
For these books your glory will ever tell.

Scrooge was puzzled by these words. He could understand the bit about "the Scrooges high and the Cratchetts low." To Ebenezer it meant that his creator—whoever it was—had decided to give the Scrooge family wealth and position but to give the Cratchett family a more humble station in life. But there were parts that made no sense to him. What were "Oliver's twists" and "Copperfield's lot"? Why did the poem talk of the creator using a pen, and what did it mean that it took only a matter of days? What was this business about the "Family heart"? Scrooge felt that if he could find out the meaning of this poem, his enjoyment of creation would be renewed and his joy in Christmas rekindled. He passed these sentiments along to his creator in a mumbled prayer as he dozed off in his chair.

Scrooge woke with a start at the stroke of midnight. The clock in his flat was chiming. He was still in his chair, and he rubbed his eyes and looked out at London through his window. But he did not see London through his window. Scrooge's attention was grabbed by the reflection on his window pane of someone standing behind him. Scrooge saw reflected on the pane a large bearded figure dressed in green fur and crowned with a wreath of holly standing in the middle of the room on a mound of fruit. He was wrapped in gifts and greenery. Scrooge's eyes went wide as he let out a frightened gasp.

"Ah, Scrooge—you're awake at last," said the figure behind him. "Turn around now and let me get a good look at you. It's been a few years."

Scrooge did as he was commanded. He slowly rose from the chair, turned himself around, and confronted the face of the Spirit of Christmas Present.

"You're looking surprisingly fit—for a man your age," said the Spirit as he began to laugh. "You haven't forgotten me, have you?"

Scrooge gathered his strength and stuttered. "No, Sir, I rem-m-m-ember you well. Are you not the Spirit of Christmas Present?"

"At your service," said the Spirit, bowing low and nearly losing the holly wreath from atop his head. "I understand that you want to restore your joy in life again—get a new grip on creation, get the luster back into your Christmas celebration. Did I get the assignment straight?"

Scrooge nodded, since words were not easily forthcoming.

"Then take my hand, Ebenezer," the Spirit commanded, stretching out his arm and fingers toward his frightened host. "We're making a couple of visits tonight that may just do the trick."

Scrooge grabbed the Spirit's hand and in the next moment found himself standing in the back of a university classroom. An animated lecture was in progress. A distinguished figure with graying hair and wild eyebrows was gesturing before a room full of attentive auditors. "Do you recognize the teacher?" the Spirit asked Scrooge.

"Yes, yes—that's old Featherby—my archaeology tutor at the academy. A great teacher. He was an expert on ancient mythology—particularly creation legends." Scrooge gazed at Mr. Featherby (who, of course, could not see Scrooge or the Spirit) and listened to his lecture. To Scrooge's amazement it was on "The Song of Creation." *Perhaps,* thought Scrooge, *I'll get the insight I need to recover my joy.*

Featherby was wrapping up his lecture by summarizing his points. "In conclusion, my young friends, this oldest of creation myths—'The Song of Creation'—cherished by a number of clans (such as the Scrooges), is a completely bogus piece of work. Contrary to the claims of the poem, we can no longer believe in an author who penned our story. There is no plot that the story of our lives follows, no hand that 'shaped each creature from head to toe.' Although the stories is definitely old and foretells (by sheer luck) the coming of the Cratchetts and the Scrooges, it is still the product of primitive minds. We now know that the stories of Oliver Twist and David Copperfield, as well as the story of the Scrooges and the Cratchetts, are products of time and chance and not some cosmic author." With that final word, Featherby dismissed the class, gathered his books, and walked briskly out of the room.

Scrooge stood in dismal silence, stunned by the words of this learned man. The Spirit merely leaned against the back wall, arms folded, legs crossed, sporting an amused grin. Scrooge finally spoke up, "What if he is right and 'The Song of Creation' is a pack of lies? Where do I go then to get my joy back?"

"And what if the moon is made of macaroni and I am merely a buttercup with a hat of holly on?" said the Spirit. "Don't play the 'what if' game with Featherby. Featherby doesn't believe in 'The Song of Creation' or in the creator it proclaims because he believes in a rival creator—the great god, Chance. Because he worships Chance, he is too narrow-minded to take 'The Song of Creation' seriously. It can't be true because it doesn't fit his faith in Chance. You won't find anything that will help you here."

With that word the Spirit stretched out his hand toward Scrooge, who grasped it tightly. The classroom disappeared and all went black.

An instant later, Scrooge was standing before a brightly lit house. The snow was falling gently around him. By the light of the gas lamp on the sidewalk Scrooge made out the name on the brass plate on the large red door: "Dickens."

The Spirit pressed his face against the front window, and Scrooge did the same, his hot breath clearing a small lens in the ice-covered pane. The parlor was filled with Christmas. A tall tree was covered with popcorn and garlands and tiny candles. Shiny packages were heaped about the tree. Scrooge saw that the room was full of children, dozens of them, playing games and laughing. Sitting in the center of the group of children, sharing in their games and laughter, was a lone adult. His high forehead glowed in the candlelight. His unkempt hair contrasted with his neatly trimmed goatee. His cheeks looked hot from his enthusiastic play with the children. A young girl in a lace-covered dress sat on his lap, and a boy stood laughing at his side.

"Who are these people, Spirit?" asked Scrooge.

"The man is Charles Dickens, and he is your creator," said the Spirit flatly. "The young girl is his niece, and the boy standing next to him is his son. The rest of the children are from a local orphanage. Listen carefully, Scrooge, for Mr. Dickens is about to tell a story."

Scrooge stared through the window again and listened. Dickens had, indeed, begun to tell a story. He called it "A Christmas Carol," and it was all about Scrooge and Marley and Bob Cratchett and Tiny Tim. Before his very eyes, Scrooge saw the story of his life being told by a man whom he had never met. If that wasn't shocking enough, when Dickens had finished, the young girl on his lap then read the poem that she had scribbled on her paper. Scrooge recognized the poem immediately. It was "The Song of Creation," word for word.

"That poem," said the Spirit, "was written by that young girl in honor of her uncle. It's her celebration of her uncle's achievement in creating the literary world of Oliver Twist, David Copperfield, and Ebenezer Scrooge."

"But that song has been in my family for years," objected Scrooge.

"I'm afraid that you are missing the point," said the Spirit, adjusting his crown of holly, which was listing to one side. "Your whole world, all of the Scrooges and Cratchetts, all of the other stories about Oliver Twist and David Copperfield were dreamed up by Dickens because of his love for the children who are gathered around him. He wrote your story, Scrooge (which, incidentally, he called *A Christmas Carol*), after visiting the orphanage where many of the children live who are here tonight."

"Do you mean to say that I am a character in a story—that the account of my humbugish life, my change of heart after meeting the three spirits of Christmas—all that was fashioned right here in this house by that man and the children he adores?" asked Scrooge with an ashen face.

"Precisely," said the Spirit, "because that is what it means to be a 'creation.' Dickens and his beloved children exist on an entirely different plane from you, so far above your story-world as to seem infinite, eternal and all-powerful in comparison—which, of course, they are."

"Spirit, though your words trouble me, I believe they are true. Tell me more about the meaning of 'The Song of Creation.' Tell me what it means to say that my story world was created because of Dickens's 'Family heart.' "

"Everything Dickens writes, whether it is *A Christmas Carol* (your story) or *Oliver Twist*, he writes out of a joy and love for his niece and son and, by association, other children. No detail of the story is left out. Every word and action in the story comes from Dickens's pen. 'From the Scrooges high to the Cratchetts low, / You shaped each creature from head to toe.' "

Scrooge was clearly puzzled, but he persevered with the conversation. "But what about the evil in the story? What about my cold heart and Jacob Marley's greed? Did Dickens create us bad? What about the line that says 'Your chapters were good from end to start'?"

"Dickens made everything in the story good. The implications of that basic truth are these: (1) you were all made by a good author, (2) he created the story out of good motives (to bring joy to his niece and son), (3) he created the story with a good goal—to bring good out of evil by rescuing you from your evil and sin, (4) you and Marley were originally good but became corrupted later, (5) nothing can take away these four kinds of goodness in Dickens's creation. Neither your evil nor Marley's can ever destroy that built-in goodness."

Scrooge spoke again. "What about the part in the Song that says, 'And when all was done you rested well, / For these books your glory will ever tell'? What does that mean?"

"It means more than just that Dickens finally finished his novels and stories and could get a good night's sleep. The poem is saying that he and the children he loves have done something of enduring value and something from which they derive endless pleasure. The 'rest' in the poem is the celebration of permanent achievement, not a nap brought on by exhaustion."

Scrooge was now silent. The Spirit took him by his hand and led him away, the house and the tree and the children fading from their sight.

When Scrooge woke up early the next morning (Christmas morning to be exact), he felt refreshed. He looked up at the window and checked the reflections from the center of the room. No figures to be seen. He stood and turned slowly around. His room seemed perfectly normal. He grabbed his coat and hat and hurried down into the bustle of the London streets.

The bookstores on Charing Cross were closed, but Scrooge stood by the windows yearning for the volumes inside. Scrooge hurried on to Piccadilly Circus. The windows of the toy shops still had the painted puppets and the shiny trains. The plump geese filled him with great satisfaction now, deeper satisfaction than before.

As he made his way home, Scrooge passed the park where he had seen the children making angels in the snow. They were at it again this Christmas day. Today one child in the flock was holding a red balloon. Scrooge stopped and watched as their bodies sank into the snow—like a coffin sinking into the earth. But just then the balloon escaped from the child's hand and began gracefully rising above the streets and spires of the dingy city, defying, for a time, the law of gravity and the atmosphere of grimness. It rose above the howls of the disappointed child, above the smoke of a thousand chimneys, curling with the smoke heavenward and out of sight.

Scrooge, suppressing a smile, gave the child a sixpence, saluted the balloon, and made his way home whistling.

The Theology Behind the Story: Creation

The parable of Scrooge begins on a note of loss. Scrooge has not misplaced his ticket or his luggage. He has lost something far more serious: his capacity for joy. His quest is simple: to find the key that will return the wide-eyed wonder of life to his soul, for "the greatest loss in life is the loss of the capacity to enjoy life."

Scrooge needs what we all need. What would it be like to experience the truths of creation in such a way that our joy and delight in God and the goodness of the life he has given to us are renewed? I want to search out with you in this chapter how the doctrine of creation might accomplish just such a work of renewal.

It's time now to add a third item to our list of worldview convictions. This third conviction (at least the first part) is concerned with the goodness and comprehensiveness of creation:

Why am I here? I am headed in the right direction when I affirm in heart and mind that the triune God has created all things, including history and culture as well as the natural world, and that they are good because God has made them.

Our comments in this chapter will focus on this crucial question of the goodness and cosmic scope of creation. I won't be discussing the issue of evolution or the meaning of the days of creation. Good discussions of that debate can be found elsewhere.[1] Instead, our question is this: What does this parable teach about the purpose and meaning of creation? The parable makes three key points.

I suggest that Scrooge's sense of loss and longing is a common one. I know it matches my own sense of longing. Can the doctrine of creation really help? Let's find out.

God and God Alone Created Everything That Exists

Central to the parable is the mysterious "Song of Creation":

Your pen scribbled long with joy and glory,
And then wrote the words that made our story;
In a matter of days you framed each plot,
From Oliver's twists to Copperfield's lot;
From the Scrooges high to the Cratchetts low,
You shaped each creature from head to toe;
Your chapters were good from end to start,
And told us much of your Family heart;
And when all was done you rested well,
For these books your glory will ever tell.

Through the Spirit of Christmas present, Scrooge discovers the meaning of this song and learns that his "creator" has fashioned a highly detailed literary world "from Oliver's twists to Copperfield's lot." In like fashion the whole spectrum of creation, from matter to Manhattan, from crustaceans to civilizations, flows from the Almighty God and his powerful word. Let's listen in on the Bible's conversation about the cosmic scope of creation that flows from the omnipotent word.

We begin by defining creation. The doctrine of creation is foundational to Christian faith. The first article of the Apostles' Creed begins with creation: "I believe in God, the Father Almighty, Maker of Heaven and Earth." So moved was Nehemiah by the truth of God as Creator that he could not restrain his worshipful enthusiasm:

> Blessed be your glorious name, and may it be exalted above all blessing and praise. You alone are the LORD. You made the heavens, even the highest heavens, and all their starry host, the earth and all that is on it, the seas and all that is in them. You give life to everything, and the multitudes of heaven worship you. (Neh 9:5-6)

Nehemiah's enthusiasm in the way he speaks of creation focuses on the fact that it was made by the word of God. Psalm 33:6 says that "by the word of the LORD were the heavens made, their starry host by the breath of his mouth." The Genesis account bears testimony to God creating by his word alone as it repeats the formula "And God said . . ."

Coupled with this creation by the word is creation out of nothing. Christianity denies that matter is eternal and affirms that it had a beginning with the creative act of God. Hebrews 11:3 speaks of this truth: "By faith we understand that the universe was formed at God's command, so that what is seen was not made out of what was visible." So important is this double truth of creation out of nothing and creation by the word that the early church fathers made it a major weapon in their defense of the faith against heretics and pagan critics. Hear Irenaeus confess the critical importance of these twin concepts:

> It is proper, then, that I should begin with the first and most important head, that is, God the creator, who made the heavens and the earth, and all things that are therein . . . and to demonstrate that there is nothing either above Him or after Him; nor that, influenced by anyone, but of His own free will He created all things, since He is the only Father, alone containing all things, and Himself commanding all things into existence.[2]

"Himself commanding all things into existence." Those are the critical words of the biblical doctrine of creation. God created by his word and out of nothing.

For evangelical faith, creation out of nothing and creation by the word of God are two crucial parts to a proper understanding of the gospel. Luther believed these twin truths were so fundamental that he regarded faith in God the Creator as that which "thoroughly determines man's salvation."[3] Luther declared as much in a sermon of 1523:

> "I believe in God the Father Almighty, creator of heaven and of earth" is, without a doubt, the highest expression of our faith. Whoever genuinely believes this has already been helped, has once again been set right, and arrived at the place from which Adam fell. Few reach the point of completely believing that He is the God who creates and makes all things. For such a man must have died to all things, to good and to evil, to death and to life, to hell and to heaven, and confess from his heart that he is able to do nothing by his own power.[4]

God creates out of nothing. For Luther this becomes a statement of who God is by nature. "God makes what he makes under the veil or form of its opposite, and therefore also *out* of its opposite. He creates life under the form of death, yes by way of death."[5]

In light of the importance of these themes of God's sovereignty and absolute creativity, we are ready to suggest a definition of creation. *Creation is the activity of the triune God in making out of nothing and by the power of his word alone everything that exists, culture as well as nature, the visible as well as the invisible, for the purpose of declaring his glory as the almighty King and eliciting in his creatures the response of glad submission and service.*

Admittedly, that is a rather lengthy definition. Let us focus on the phrase "everything that exists, culture as well as nature, the visible as well as the invisible." This phrase affirms that the creation is absolutely comprehensive in its scope. Such an affirmation warns Christians against adhering to dualism in any of its forms. Let's look at Genesis 1 and the way it depicts the fullness of creation's scope.

First of all, Genesis one teaches that *God creates the sphere of matter.* I take Genesis 1:1 to be the topic sentence of the chapter, and 1:2 to refer to the first stage of the creation process. Not all commentators want to do that.

Some consider that because the phrase in verse 1 "the heavens and the earth" always refers to an orderly cosmos, verse 2 must represent some prior stage of life before creation. This seems to be unnecessary. Even granting that the phrase "the heavens and the earth" refers to an orderly cosmos, verse 2 can be seen as part of the process of creating that order. This becomes more plausible when verse 2 is understood less as chaos and more as the origin of matter in raw, unshaped form. I appreciate Albert Wolters's insight into 1:2, that the expression "formless and empty" is not a statement of chaos but rather "describes the first step toward the order of the earthly cosmos, something like the preliminary rough sketch of the artist, which is later filled in with color and detail, or like the bare frame of a house before it is finished and furnished."[6]

Genesis 1:2 then should be seen as an affirmation that God made all matter. Atoms and electrons come into existence by his powerful word. I like the image painted by Thomas Watson: "God brought all this glorious fabric of the world out of the womb of nothing."[7] This has sometimes been referred to by theologians as the first creation.

Second, note that Genesis chapter 1 teaches that *God creates the sphere of nature.* But there is a second creation as well. Just as God made matter, he also ordered it. Genesis 1:3ff. gives a description of this second level of creation. Thomas Watson links the creation of matter and the creation of order:

> God made this lump and mass . . . and then beautified it. He divided the sea and the earth, he decked the earth with flowers, the trees with fruit; but what is beauty when it is masked over? Therefore, that we might behold this glory, God made the light. The heavens were bespangled with the sun, moon and stars, so that the world's beauty might be beheld and admired. God, in the creation, began with things less noble and excellent, rocks and vegetables; and then the rational creatures, angels and men.[8]

The ordering of creation took place in the six days and involved creating spheres or kingdoms (days 1-3) and then filling them with rulers or kings to govern the spheres (days 4-6). Thus all of nature is created by God just as certainly as all of matter is.

Third, we can see in Genesis 1 that *God creates the sphere of culture.* But Genesis 1 does not limit the scope of creation just to matter and nature. Human culture is created by the word of God and must be included in the comprehensive sweep of creation. The creative word of God that brings culture into being is given by God in Genesis 1:28:

> God blessed them and said to them, "Be fruitful and increase in number; fill the earth and subdue it. Rule over the fish of the sea and the birds of the air and over every living creature that moves on the ground."

This third creation is sometimes called the "creation mandate" or the "cultural mandate." Some people object that the cultural mandate marks a different element in Genesis 1 and should not be seen as part of God's creation. This seems to be an arbitrary objection. Consider the word *toledoth,* which appears repeatedly throughout the book of Genesis to introduce major new sections of the book. In Genesis 2:4 the word means the generation of something or the producing of something. Genesis 2:4 opens with the statement that the *generations* of the heavens and earth (NRSV) are to be given. What follows? A discussion of the beginnings of human culture, the beginnings of marriage, the tending of the garden—these are the things that follow the "beginnings of the heavens and earth." What does this mean? It simply supports the central place in the doctrine of creation of the origin of human culture as the third circle of creation after matter and nature. As Wolters writes:

> The creation mandate provides a sort of climax to the six days of creation. The stage is set by the stage director, the actors are introduced, and as the curtain rises and the stage director moves backstage, they are given their opening cue. The drama of human history is about to begin, and the first and foundational Word of God to his children is the command to "fill and subdue."[9]

This point is important for the formation of a biblical worldview, says Wolters. "Creation is not something that, once made, remains a static quantity. There is . . . an unfolding of creation."[10]

It is also important to include the work of human culture in the goodness of creation. We hear God's pronouncement in Genesis 1:31 that after completing the work of creation (matter, nature, and culture) "God saw all that he had made, and it was very good." Dualism is refuted when we insist on the comprehensiveness of creation.

Fourth, the Bible in other places teaches that *God creates the sphere of spirit.* The scope of creation would not be complete without making mention of the creation of the spiritual world. Colossians 1:16 speaks of Christ's creation of invisible rulers and authorities. John 1:1-3 declares that Christ created all things. Psalm 148:2-5 teaches that angels, like everything else in God's world, were created by his hand. While we deny as without basis the claim of Mormons and others that human souls preexist, we do affirm that the spiritual realm is completely the creation of God. The purpose of angels is the same as the purpose for everything else in creation—to serve God and declare his glory (Col 1:16; Ps 148:5).

Finally, we must conclude from the above that *the creation is cosmic in its scope.* We've seen that this feature of the parable mirrors an important biblical truth. God's creation is cosmic and all-encompassing. We need to break out of the limited thinking that would restrict God's creation to the areas explored by natural science. Art, business, politics and religion as well as physics, geology, biology and zoology are all disciplines that explore God's good creation. We must fight dualism on this fundamental level, the dualism that would narrow the field of God's creative sovereignty to some parts of reality and not all. The doctrine of creation enables us to say wholeheartedly with Paul, "For everything God created is good, and nothing is to be rejected" (1 Tim 4:4). But now we have moved beyond the question of scope and have raised the issue of creation's goodness. We need to take a closer look at that important question.

God's Creation Is Good
The climax of the parable is reached when Scrooge finds out the real reason why the world of *A Christmas Carol* exists:

"I'm afraid that you are missing the point," said the Spirit, adjusting his crown of holly, which was listing to one side. "Your whole world, all of the Scrooges and Cratchetts, all of the other stories about Oliver Twist and David Copperfield were dreamed up by Dickens because of his love for the children who are gathered around him."

Creation is at heart the Trinity in an act of family celebration. That's what the parable teaches anyway. What does the Word of God say?

God tells us clearly that his creation is good. Seven times in Genesis 1 we hear God's repeated verdict that he is pleased with his creation and hence exults in its goodness (Gen 1:4, 10, 18, 21, 25, 31). Says theologian James Garrett: "Against all dualisms that would make the created order to be evil or the product of an evil or angry deity, be they Marcionite, Gnostic or Manichaean, the Christian teaching has insisted on the goodness of creation."[11] The New Testament reaffirms the conviction of creation's goodness introduced in Genesis 1: "for everything God created is good, and nothing is to be rejected" (1 Tim 4:4). Nothing that God has made, whether matter, nature, or culture, can be inherently evil. I'd like to elaborate on this under three headings.

The first point about the goodness of Creation concerns the trinitarian purpose of creation. Psalm 19 reminds us that creation exists to declare God's glory. That is the essential purpose of creation. In light of the reality of the Trinity we can see that the goodness of creation is its usefulness in expressing the Trinity's glory, that is, its mutual love—honoring, exalting, and enjoying one another. While humankind is led to exult in and enjoy God by encountering God's work in creating matter, nature, and history, all creation has an inextinguishable goodness because God derives delight from it within his triune family life. Listen to how Colossians 1:15-16 describes the Father's delight in exalting the Son through creation:

> He is the image of the invisible God, the firstborn over all creation. For by him all things were created: things in heaven and on earth, visible and invisible, whether thrones or powers or rulers or authorities; all things were created by him and for him.

Hebrews 1:2 and John 1:3 make parallel points about the Son's role in creation. But Colossians 1:16 is most explicit in telling us the purpose of creation. Creation is *for* him, not only *by* him. This must mean that the exaltation of the Son by the Father and Spirit is the intended purpose of creation. The Son's response at the end of history will be to return the glory he has received and exalt the Father and live (as always) in glad submission to him (1 Cor 15:28). Thus creation is good in that it has as its meaning and purpose the Trinity's glory and good pleasure. Creation is good, and indestructibly good, because it is made by and for Christ. Those two facts cannot change, hence the goodness of creation cannot change.

A second point about the goodness of creation is that it is repeatedly under attack. Not everybody shares the conviction that all the creation is good. *Dualism* is the name we give to views that would regard some parts of creation as morally inferior to others and imply a limit of God's lordship over his creation. The most prominent expression of this dualism in Christian circles was a second-century heresy called Gnosticism. Albert Wolters describes the Gnostic dualism that sought to blame a flawed creation for suffering and sin (thereby deflecting moral responsibility from human will and human action):

> In the early church there was a heresy called Gnosticism that denied the goodness of creation in a fundamental way. It held that the Creator of Genesis 1 was a subordinate deity who had rebelled against the supreme good God, and that the world he made was an evil place, a prison from which people had to be rescued. . . . Against the Gnostic maligning of God's creation (or some part of it) [the Christian] must proclaim the goodness of all creation.[12]

Gnosticism did not die with the close of the second century. The values of Gnosticism and some of the perspectives of Gnosticism entered Western civilization and have risen to the surface time and again under a hundred names. The fundamental mentality remains the same, however. Superspiritual types like the Gnostics see creation and humanity as an abortion—an accident that must be righted. Whatever is wrong with the world is traceable to flawed origins, not a subsequent fall. Anders Nygren reminds us that there are both vulgar and "heavenly" versions of gnosticism. Viewing creation as trash to avoid and viewing it as trash to play with both betray a common error: the perception that the world outside of me is basically junk. The one good is the self. Rejection of creation or indulgence in creation can be good if it leads to self-transcendence. In our age of self-absorption, creation can be seen as good only to the degree that it serves my personal need to be exalted or fulfilled, and it becomes "evil" or worthless if it does not serve my needs or fulfill my wishes. Creation's goodness is lost by selfist (or gnostic) perspectives on life.13

Many expressions of the selfist or gnostic mentality exist today. Gnosticism might be reflected in the Christian who will not engage in certain cultural activities because they are felt to be inherently evil. The feminist who regards history as junk because it is written by men or is reducible to the story of the oppression of women may be reflecting the attack on creation that comes from the selfist/gnostic way of thinking. The Marxist who rejects middle-class bourgeois culture because it reinforces the status quo could be reflecting the attack on creation. The rationalist who rejects the goodness of the "supernatural" or spiritual parts of creation and the mystic who rejects the material aspects—both want to blame creation and junk aspects of it and may be playing into the hands of a selfist worldview.

But biblical religion is not the least bit embarrassed by creation. The world, history, and culture are to be seen as projects of God over which he takes full responsibility (Gen 1; Is 40; Col 1). Whatever is wrong with the world has absolutely nothing to do with origins, but has only to do with a moral act of treason by the first man and woman after creation occurred.

A third point about the goodness of creation involves learning to distinguish between structure and direction. What do we make of the presence of sin and evil in the world? Hasn't evil ruined the original goodness of creation? Scrooge asks about that at one point in the parable.

Scrooge was clearly puzzled, but he persevered with the conversation. "But what about the evil in the story? What about my cold heart and Jacob Marley's greed? Did Dickens create us bad? What about the line that says 'Your chapters were good from end to start'?"

Has sin ruined creation and removed its original goodness? I would insist, on the basis of Scripture, that the goodness of creation is indestructible despite the sinful use of creation by a fallen humanity. Two terms, *structure* and *direction*, may help us understand the problem of evil in creation. *Structure* refers to the inherent goodness of creation—it is good because it is made by God for his glory. That never changes. As Wolters has said, "God does not make junk and he does not junk what he has made." *Direction* refers to how the creatures use God's gifts of matter, nature, and culture. Do they use them for God or for idols? Do they use these good gifts for true worship or for the traitorous evil of apostasy and idolatry? In a fallen world humankind can only misuse God's creation (that is, not use it for the intended purpose of glorifying Christ). Structural goodness remains, however. Matter is still made *by* God and *for* God even if it is shamelessly misdirected by fallen hearts and hands. Thus while Christians reject all forms of dualism, they affirm a crucial antithesis.

What is this antithesis? The antithesis is religious and moral, not creational and structural. All things were intended to be used for the worship of the triune God. That is the right use of all things. The moral antithesis of that right use is the sin of idolatry. This is the religious antithesis that cuts across all created reality. Prayer and preaching can be just as directionally wicked as business and moviemaking might be. Or these things can be just as directionally good if they are done for the glory of God. But all are structurally good, because they are made by and for God. That origin and destiny never change.

Therefore, "The Song of Creation" was right:

Your chapters were good from end to start,
And told us much of your Family heart;
And when all was done you rested well,
For these books your glory will ever tell.

That might not be great poetry, but it is good theology. God has made everything, and everything is indestructibly good.

The Truths of Creation Can Restore Our Joy in God and the Life He Has Given Us in Christ

By the end of the parable Scrooge has found again his love and joy in creation and in Christmas. It would be unrealistic to suggest that a little reading in the doctrine of creation could have the kind of renewing impact on our lives that it did on Scrooge. But it is no exaggeration to say that once the truths of creation make their way into our heart and begin to shape our worldview, we have every reason to expect that joy and delight in God will increase. What specific effects would a rediscovery of the truths of creation bring? Joy in God's person, joy in God's gift of life, and joy in God's great gift of redemption are three primary possibilities. But before we look at these benefits of the doctrine of creation, we need to mention something of the covenantal nature of creation.

Creation is nothing more or less than the kingdom of God. All that we have said points to this. The universe is God's temple or palace, and all that transpires in his kingdom is intended to glorify him as King of Kings. This clearly implies that we are meant to be more than interested or amused bystanders watching creation unfold. We are obligated by the trinitarian nature of created reality (i.e., everything is made by the triune God and for the triune God) to live lives of glad submission to God.

The law of love (Mk 12:29-31) is the law of God's creation-kingdom; it is the very warp and woof of created reality. Whether it means submitting to the laws of physics or art or education—the law of love as the law of the kingdom is pervasive throughout creation. We are to love God totally and others unselfishly. This general law is expressed in a thousand applications (or in our fallen world, broken in a thousand ways). Recovering or discovering (for the first time) the meaning of creation can be the first step (but not the only step) to deepening that love and the glad submission to God that he desires. Let's look at how such a view of creation as I have presented here can help to renew our joy in God.

Creation can renew our joy in the person of God. Jonathan Edwards believed that the ultimate purpose of creation was not to fall in love with creation but to increase our longing and love for the Creator. Creation is but the shining or emanation of God's triune glory in eternity. When we see the light of God's beauty in the face of creation, our joy in God should increase:

> The emanation or communication of the divine fullness, consisting in the knowledge of God, love to him, and joy in him, has relation both to God and the creature: but it has relation to God as its fountain, as the thing communicated is something of its internal fullness. The water in the stream is something of the fountain; and the beams of the sun are something of the sun. And again, they have relation to God as their object: for the knowledge communicated is the knowledge of God; and the love communicated is the love of God; and the happiness communicated is the happiness of God. In the creature's knowing, esteeming, loving, rejoicing in, and praising God, the glory of God is both exhibited and acknowledged; his fullness is received and returned. . . . The beams of glory come from God, are something of God, and are refunded back again to their original. So that the whole is of God, and in God, and to God; and he is the beginning, and the middle and the end.[14]

By turning to his creation and looking at it with new eyes—not as a resource to exploit or junk to get rid of but as a word-picture from God, a communication of his love and beauty—my love and joy are stirred and my desire for God is increased. Psalm 104:31-34 shows that the praise of God's work in creation leads to a glad exaltation of the person of God:

> May the glory of the Lord endure forever;
> may the Lord rejoice in his works—
> he who looks at the earth, and it trembles,
> who touches the mountains, and they smoke.
> I will sing to the Lord all my life;
> I will sing praise to my God as long as I live.
> May my meditation be pleasing to him,
> as I rejoice in the Lord.

Creation can renew our joy in the good life God has given us. James Houston writes of the Puritan George Traherne, who developed the high art of enjoying God through his creation. Traherne drew endless pleasure from God's works.

> "Your enjoyment of the world is never right," wrote Traherne, "till every morning you awake in Heaven; see yourself in your Father's palace; and look upon the skies, the earth, and the air as Celestial Joys: having such a reverend esteem of all, as if you were among the Angels."[15]

Houston notes how much like a pantheist Traherne sounds. But Traherne was spiritually shrewd. He knew that the worship of creation led, after the initial rush of carnal joy, to a dreary bondage, selfish ambition, or a godless consumer mentality that would eventually drain away one's joy in creation. Joy in creation comes from enjoying God as the giver of the good gifts of this life, not from idolizing the creation as a substitute for God. Traherne wrote of enjoying God's creation that

> above all trades, above all occupations, this is the most sublime. This is the greatest of affairs. Whatever else we do it is only in order that we may live conveniently and to enjoy the world and God within it; which is the sovereign employment including and crowning all the celestial life of a glorious creature, without which all other estates are servile and impertinent.[16]

Houston's assessment of Traherne is full of insight:

> In contrast to this sentiment, how imprisoned Traherne would view modern man, caught up in the idolatries of tyrannical professionalism, and such pragmatism of spirit, that instead of seeing creation with a childlike and overwhelming delight, sees it only as data for the

intellect, and as resources for consumption.[17]

To see creation correctly is not to work at one's job or at one's play with that "quiet desperation" that Thoreau wrote about. To see creation correctly is to work and play as one whose whole life is a gift and whose present and future are in the hands of a good and great God.

Creation can renew our joy in the restoration of the creation in Christ. As we will see in our final chapter, a lively, all-encompassing view of creation can deepen our joy in the cross of Christ and the redemption that it has accomplished. Salvation is not escape from creation but the restoration of creation. Both doctrines suffer irreparable loss when they are divorced. Each experiences new freshness and vitality when they are joined. The cross becomes a greater delight and wonder to me when I consider that it restored the whole cosmos:

> For God was pleased to have all his fullness dwell in him, and through him to reconcile to himself all things, whether things on earth or things in heaven, by making peace through his blood, shed on the cross. (Col 1:19-20)

Conclusion

Conviction number three (introduced in the first chapter) has been our focus in this chapter: "Why am I here? I am headed in the right direction when I affirm in heart and mind that the triune God has created all things, including history and culture as well as the natural world, and that they are good because God has made them."

Scrooge's story and God's reliable Word have both pointed toward this great conviction. Three points from the parable and from the Scriptures have been explored. First, we affirmed that God made everything by his word. Matter, nature, and culture, things visible and invisible, make up the cosmic scope of creation. All forms of dualism must be rejected. Second, we affirmed that God made everything good. The goodness of creation consists of the triune God using this cosmos of matter, nature, and culture as a way to celebrate his family life of mutual deference and delight. Third, we affirmed that the truths of creation can restore our joy in God and the life he has given us in creation and in Christ. Creation is covenantal—leading me into glad submission. From the perspective of glad submission, creation fuels my delight in God's person, God's gifts, and God's work of salvation.

Scrooge's longing is my own. As I move past the debate about creation and into the truths of creation's goodness and scope, my joy in God the Almighty Creator is stirred. A lightness comes to my step as words of gratitude come to my lips. But my gratitude should not just focus on God's original work of *making* this world of wonder. God deserves additional praise for *sustaining* and *governing* it too. Those two words describe the biblical truth of God's providence, and that is what we will take up in the next chapter with some friends named Huck and Jim.

Questions for Individuals or for Group Discussion

Part One
1. What is Scrooge's personal interest in unlocking the mystery of creation?

Do you agree with the statement "The greatest loss in life is the loss of the capacity to enjoy life"?

How can rediscovering creation renew one's joy?

How can it renew the meaning of redemption?

2. Creation can be defined as "the work of God in bringing into being, without the use of any preexisting materials, everything that is" (Millard Erickson, *Christian Theology,* 366). How does the parable deal with creation out of nothing and creation by the word of God?

What biblical support can be found for those two notions?

3. "The Song of Creation" bears some resemblance to Genesis 1. What similarities can you identify?

How does the Song deal with the cosmic scope of creation?

Does the Song clearly reject dualism? Explain.

4. How does the parable defend the goodness of creation?

Does the corruption of sin destroy the goodness of creation? Explain.

How does grasping the goodness of creation renew Scrooge?

How would it renew someone today who has grown weary of life?

5. What was Featherby's position on creation?

What are some of the leading rivals to the biblical view of creation?

6. Some theologians bring out the importance of the Creator-creature distinction, emphasizing that all proper theology must begin with the

radical otherness and superiority of God to humanity. How does the parable bring out this Creator-creature distinction?

What role does the doctrine of God's attributes play in bringing out this distinction?

7. What is the ultimate reason for the creation of *A Christmas Carol* according to the parable?

Orthodoxy talks of creation *from* the Father, *through* the Son and *by* the Holy Spirit. How does the parable address the distinctive roles of each person of the Trinity?

What did the song mean when it said that the "chapters" of creation "told us much of your Family heart"?

Part Two

8. Review the definition of creation. Does this definition safeguard the doctrine of creation from the errors of atheism, deism, pantheism and polytheism? How?

What are the implications of denying creation out of nothing or creation out of the word?

9. The scope of creation is said to include matter, nature, and culture. What are the reasons given for including culture?

How does such a view of creation's scope offer some protection against the inroads of dualism?

What is your personal evaluation of this view?

10. What does the author mean when he says that creation is covenantal?

What kind of response should the truths of creation produce in the believer?

11. In what ways does creation deepen our enjoyment of the Trinity? of redemption?

Do believers sometimes fall into the trap of seeing salvation as an escape from creation rather than the restoration of creation? Give examples for your answers.

12. How would you defend the goodness of creation and culture in a fallen world?

How do the concepts of structure and direction help?

13. How would you describe the importance of the doctrine of creation to you currently?

How would you use the truths of this doctrine to minister to God's people in a local church setting?

in a campus setting?

in the home?

in the office?

For Further Reading

I recommend Henri Blocher's *In the Beginning* (Downers Grove, Ill.: IVP, 1987) and James Houston's *I Believe in the Creator* (London: Hodder and Stoughton, 1978). Blocher is somewhat controversial but attempts to look at Genesis 1—4 from the perspective of biblical theology rather than the debate with science. Houston's book is a creative look at the same material with fresh insights throughout. Two additional resources for those wanting to delve more deeply into the debates about origins would be Michael Denton's *Evolution: A Theory in Crisis* (London: Burnet Books, 1985) and *The Christian Scholar's Review* 21 (September 1991); this special issue is devoted to the debate within evangelicalism about creation, evolution and Christian faith. The contributions by Alvin Plantinga and Pattle Pun are particularly noteworthy.

Chapter Six
Providence:
Huck and Jim
Meet Their Author

Huck and Jim decided they'd had enough of civilization once again, so they set out in the dark of one summer night down the river. This time they were both going to South America, and they were going to raft as far as New Orleans and then sign on to some ship headed south from there. Seemed like a good plan, but this journey was a lot more dangerous than the one they had taken before. It wasn't just the Indians and thieves and slave traders. They encountered a good heap of trouble from kinds like that. But just a day's float from New Orleans they came up against something that caught them way off guard. They met their author.

First hint they had that he was coming was a letter they got. How do you get letters when you're floating in the middle of the Mississippi? They pulled in to shore one day and happened to go for a sasparilla at the Grand Hotel and right there on the letter board as they came into the lobby was a letter, big as life, with the words "Huck and Jim" written right on the envelope. Huck looked around, a bit timidly, then grabbed the envelope, tore it open and read the letter out loud, on the spot, to Jim.

Dear Huck and Jim,

Greetings to my two favorite characters. How have things been going? I'll meet you in the dining room of this here hotel at 1 p.m. We'll be traveling together to New Orleans. Till then I remain your loving author,

Mark Twain

You can be sure that Huck and Jim were there at 1 p.m. in the dining room. As they scanned the crowd they noticed a striking gentleman with a thick, curly crop of white hair, a bushy mustache curved down around the corners of his mouth, and a huge Cuban cigar jutting from the ledge of his lips. He was dressed in a white suit and seemed to be dreaming about something, for as Huck and Jim approached and stood silently by the table, the white-maned man didn't notice until Huck coughed.

"Huck and Jim," the man said warmly, standing to greet them, "I've really been looking forward to this! Have a seat."

Without comment but with a great deal of uneasiness, the two river adventurers sat down. After an awkward minute of silence Huck burst out, loud enough to turn the heads of the whole room full of dinner guests, "Who in tarnation are you and what do want with us?"

The great white figure leaned forward and gave Huck a hard stare. "You know me, Huck; I'm your author, your creator. I wrote you into existence, I am now writing you into continuing existence, and I intend to keep writing you into a future existence."

Jim spoke: "Sir, I don't know who'd you are, but I'm willin' to listen t'what you got ta say. How's bout you, Huck?" Huck gave some sort of grunt and kept his gaze on the mysterious stranger in white.

"The long and the short of it, Jim and Huck," the stranger said, "is that you are characters in a story that I've created. You're getting towards the end of the story now, and I wanted to let you know that."

"You mean to say," said Huck, "that every part of this story, the people, the time, the encounters, the dangers, suffering, escapes, emotions, setting and everything are simply inventions of your mind and not real?"

"They are inventions, Huck," Twain replied. "I've created, governed, and sustained everything in the story (including your surprised look and madly thumping heart). But you are wrong to say that you, Jim and the story are not real. You're real characters in a real story with real twists and suspense. You're not real in Hartford or St. Louis like I and my family are in my world as an author. Nevertheless, you are as real as I made you to be. No more and no less."

It was Jim's turn to look puzzled now. With terror in his eyes, he looked at Twain and said, "You mean I ain't never goin' to be free? I been runnin' from slavery all my life, and there was always the hope of gettin' north or makin' our way to Brazil or someplace, and then I'd be free at last. But you sayin' I'm the kind of slave that can't be freed. The only freedom I'd ever find in this story of yours would be a phony freedom. Jus' be kiddin' myself."

Twain's large, aged eyes welled up. He tried to clear his throat but could only speak with a trembling voice. "Jim, don't you understand, your freedom is real because it is given. Your freedom is one of the first gifts I gave to every character in my story. Although they struggle and suffer, they get to follow and achieve their heart's desire. That's the only kind of freedom there is, doing or seeking what your heart wants the most. I wrote the two of you together because you wanted to be together; I'm writing you down the Mississippi because that's where your heart desires to go; I'm writing you safely to New Orleans because that's where your deepest desires draw you."

"But those desires were implanted by you. They aren't ours," Huck said with anger.

Twain banged his huge fist hard on the linen-covered table. "Don't you understand—the only desires that exist in a character are 'implanted' ones. I gave you the gift of freedom—the only kind of freedom that exists—the gift of doing what you desire. There is no 'you' apart from me. I give you life and breath and desire, and all I hear you say is that you, as a character, don't want character traits, you want to be the ultimate author."

"But," said Huck with mounting defiance, "what about the wrong desires that we find ourselves struggling with, what about the evil desires that fuel the actions and fill the hearts of the con-men, slave-dealers and crooks that we've kept coming up against all through this story? Are you the author of this evil, creating it and implanting it in your characters' hearts and then punishing them for doing what you made them do?"

Twain looked down at his cigar and put it out in the ashtray. He folded his hands and sat still for a while. He spoke slowly. "When I began this story I had one purpose in mind—to celebrate my family. Within our circle of love there in our Hartford home I have known joy the likes of which I have never imagined possible. Out of our love, family times, and evenings of good conversation this story was born. The story exists to exalt the people in my family whom I love, and I have chosen to exalt them by drawing contrasts. The shifting, suffering, survival kind of life that you and Jim have is the opposite of our close, secure life within the family circle. Each evening as we read the next events in your story, there wells up within us a fresh appreciation for what we have, a renewed sense of the precious gift that a loving family is and, most surprisingly, a desire to share our family life with those who do not have it so well."

"But you haven't answered my question," Huck said with irritation. "How can you punish people for being the way you made them?"

"I'm getting there," Twain answered. "The evil within the story is a permitted evil. When I created Pap, your drunken father, I left out of him my real heart. It's what I didn't implant that made possible the seed of evil in his heart. He was created a good character, but the logic of his heart guided my pen to direct his development in the way it went. One of my rules as an author has always been to create and sustain the integrity, the heart's desire of each character. I write the whole story based on the desires that flow out of the heart of each character. The real big river in this story is not the Mississippi but the current generated by each character's psyche. So the real implanting of evil is the sowing that each character does in the lives of others in the story. My 'sovereignty' as author over the story flows through the channels cut by my characters' hungry hearts. I decided to withhold my family love from Pap and then watched to see what he would do even as I created him.

"I had already purposed to bring joy to my own family through this story, whether by reflecting our love or contrasting it or a combination of both. We decided as a family to go with the combination. What of the punishment that I will bring into the lives of the characters that I permitted to play evil roles in this story? I will carry the story to its just resolve and let the hearts' desires be fulfilled. Those who pursued selfish ends will be given up to their selfishness. Those who pursued the liberation of others will be liberated. Each character will reap what each has sown. If that sounds unfair to you, then I suggest we drop the discourse altogether."

Huck and Jim had hardly touched the food that had been silently laid in front of them during the course of the conversation. Huck stirred his peas around on the plate and said, "All what you're saying, Mr. Twain, would be a whole lot easier to take if I knew your heart."

What Twain was about to say will never be known, for at that instant two men, both carrying guns, bulled their way into the dining room. "There's the nigger," yelled the taller of the two men. "Shoot if he moves."

Huck and Jim sat paralyzed as the two men approached the table. Without turning his head, Twain whispered instructions. "When I say 'now,' you and Jim hightail it for the rear door. Head straight for the raft, and when you get there, push off for New Orleans and don't stop till you get to wharf twelve."

The men were about ten feet away when Twain yelled "Now!" Huck and Jim took off for the door as Twain turned the table over on the men, blocking their line of fire. Huck pushed Jim through the door and glanced back in time to see the two men empty their ammunition in Twain's chest. The great white figure's face was disfigured, his white suit red with blood, and his body draped backwards over the upturned table.

Huck and Jim ran to the raft and poled quickly out into the main current as curls of fog rose to veil their escape. They moved with the great river and soon felt that their own emotions were part of the snaking current that drew them rapidly toward New Orleans.

By morning, pink outlines of buildings, wharves, and boats of every size confirmed that they had made it. They guided their primitive craft along the wharves and pulled in to number twelve. They tied up and jumped onto the wharf and then stopped in their tracks. There before them was the most beautiful family they had ever seen. The mother was decked out in the finest silks; the daughters, gleaming with intelligence and good humor, stood beside her. But dwarfing them all, and standing with mustache twitched upwards to make room for a smile as wide as the river, was Twain. His suit was white and unstained. His face was flushed with life and warmth.

Huck spoke first: "How'd you get here? I saw you draped over the table back at the Grand Hotel." Jim was shaking, certain that he was seeing a ghost.

Twain reared back his head and roared. "The story's over, Huck and Jim."

"What do you mean?" Huck demanded.

"You're now in my world. You've entered the world of the Author; this is my real family, who helped bring you into existence and who cried and laughed at your antics throughout the story-period of your life. You and Jim are now part of our real family. We've adopted you and are bringing you back to Hartford."

Jim and Huck looked at each other in disbelief. "This some kind o' trick, Mr. Twain?" Jim asked.

"No trick, Jim," Twain answered, "The violent scene you saw at the Grand Hotel was part of the story. I was actually writing that in Hartford while it was going on in the story."

Huck dropped his head a little and began pushing one foot around in small circles on the wharf.

Twain spoke again: "I know what you're thinking, Huck. You thought that my dying for you back at the Hotel proved my good intentions, proved that my love for the characters in my story was real. And now you think that it was phony because I was sitting cozy in my study in Hartford."

Twain's wife grew pale at her husband's comments and interrupted him. "Darling, what are you saying? You know that when you wrote that scene, you were barely able to hold your pen."

She turned to Huck and Jim and continued. "My husband wrote this story for the joy of our family. As he wrote, as he created this literary universe, he poured the love that our family generated into that story-world. He suffered when Pap became a drunk and beat your mother, Huck. He suffered as we all did when you were treated so badly for being a slave, Jim. But it took him months to write the scene in the Grand Hotel. It brought a separation into our family, so great was the empathy he felt for the two of you. He would spend days alone. That separation from his loved ones was caused by the two of you and that confrontation at the hotel.

"He may have written it in a story-world, but it surely sent shock waves through our family world in Hartford. His love for you is real, because he allowed himself to love you with the same kind of love he has for me and the children. Though you were only characters, you were loved like family, and that is why we are here today—to take you home with us forever." After saying this, Twain's wife covered her face in her hands and wept.

The girls surrounded Huck and Jim, each grabbing an arm, and escorted them off the wharf to the waiting coach. The great author and his wife came behind them more slowly. Huck thought he noticed a slight limp in Twain's gait and one hand clutching his chest as though covering an old but cherished wound.

The Theology Behind the Story: Providence

The doctrine of God's providential control should be a comfort. How reassuring to know, we are told, that in a world that seems to be falling apart, God is still in charge. But not everyone responds that way to the truth of God's providence. Take Huck Finn, for instance. In the parable, Huck doesn't like the logic of providence. The creator's control of his life bothers him more than it comforts him. Right in the middle of an exciting adventure he discovers that he's made of ink and paper and some Hartford author is in control of the whole show. He becomes angry. His freedom seems threatened, which to him means that the goodness of the author is in question. There are Christians today who feel the same as Huck did about the idea of providence.

I'd like to look at the doctrine of providence in light of both the comforts and the concerns that this teaching arouses. My own conviction is that the comforts of providence far outweigh the concerns and can increase our joy in God. But we need to understand the doctrine before we can reach comforting conclusions. The parable makes three affirmations that can help us understand and even appreciate the truth of God's providential leadership of his world.

Providence Teaches That God Controls Everything That Happens in a Way Consistent with His Glory and Our Freedom

Huck gives a pretty mangled definition of providence in the form of a question that he asks Twain: "You mean to say," said Huck, "that every part of this story, the people, the time, the encounters, the dangers, suffering, escapes, emotions, setting and everything are simply inventions of your mind and not real?" Jim adds that the idea of an author being in total control of his story is another form of slavery. Twain tries to correct Huck and Jim by asserting that the only freedom and meaning they have in the story exist *because* of his authorship, not in spite of it. This gets all the more complicated when one looks at the issue of evil and suffering in a world controlled by God. Who's right?

What I need to do now is state the doctrine positively and biblically. I'd like to make five statements about what the doctrine of providence teaches (and how it squares with miracles and human freedom). Then we will see how God's providence relates to evil and suffering.

I observe first of all that *providence has a plan*. Providence has a prologue. It is called God's decree (or plan). The decree of God logically precedes the providential rule of God over his unfolding creation. Millard Erickson defines God's decree as "his eternal decision rendering certain all things which shall come to pass."[1] The Old Testament teaches the fact of God's decree, employing several words to do so. *Yatsar* is used to convey the idea that God determines and plans things beforehand (cf. Ps 139:16; Is 22:11; 37:26; 46:11). *Ya'ats* and *'etsah* are used repeatedly in the Old Testament to illustrate the same concept. In the New Testament, God's plan is said to be behind the creation and preservation of the cosmos (Rev 4:11); the salvation of individuals (Rom 9:15, 16; Eph 1:11); the sufferings of Christ (Lk 22:42; Acts 2:23; 1 Pet 1:20); humanity's life and destiny (Acts 18:21; Rom 15:32; Jas 4:5); and the smallest details of life (Mt 10:29). The words of the Westminster Confession of Faith summarize the biblical teaching about the divine decree: "God from all eternity did by the most wise and holy counsel of his own will freely and unchangeably ordain whatsoever comes to pass" (chapter 3, section 1). The execution of God's plan involves the action of providence.

Second, *providence is defined as sovereign control*. I like the definition of providence given by Twain when he spoke of governing everything in the story. That seems to be what the Bible teaches. Consider the following sampler of biblical texts that speak to the scope and content of the doctrine of providence:

☐ Psalm 115:3—"He does whatever pleases him."

☐ Matthew 10:29 (of sparrows)—"Not one of them will fall to the ground apart from the will of your Father."

☐ Job 12:23-24—"He makes nations great, and destroys them; he enlarges nations, and disperses them. He deprives the leaders of the earth of their reason; he sends them wandering through a trackless waste."

☐ Psalm 22:28—"Dominion belongs to the LORD and he rules over the nations."

☐ Daniel 4:17—"The Most High is sovereign over the kingdoms of men and gives them to anyone he wishes and sets over them the lowliest of men."

☐ Isaiah 46:9-10—"I am God and there is no other. . . . I will do all that I please."

We could go on multiplying texts. The point of the above passages seems clear enough. God is in control of the story of creation. Nature, culture, history, humanity, salvation, damnation—nothing escapes his providential rule. But these passages push us to make some more distinctions about the doctrine of providence. Three parts of providence are seen: God rules (governance), God cares and provides (sustenance), and God uses means (concurrence).

Third, providence teaches that *God rules*. God's governing of his creation may be defined as "that continued activity of God whereby he rules all things teleologically [i.e., in light of his ultimate purpose] so as to secure the accomplishment of the divine purpose."[2] God's rule of his world flows from the doctrine of creation and extends to the doctrine of last things. God is the King of Kings who has fashioned for himself a kingdom to display his glory. This aspect of providence stresses that God shapes all events to reveal his glory. "Providence is the beneficent outworking of God's sovereignty whereby all events are directed and disposed to bring about the purposes and glory and good for which the universe was made."[3] Psalm 22:28 speaks of this kingly dimension when it declares that "dominion belongs to the LORD and he rules over the nations."

What is this glory of God that history conspires to reveal? I mentioned in the last chapter that the purpose of creation was the mutual delight of the Trinity: the Father exalting and enjoying the Son, the Son exalting and enjoying the Father and the Spirit, and the Spirit exalting and enjoying the Father and the Son. In other words, God's purpose in governing history is to express his joy and love for each of the persons within the triune family. The exaltation of the Trinity through the kingdom of God (the whole history of the cosmos from creation through redemption to final consummation) is the purpose behind providence.

Thus everything that happens in the human story will contribute to this great end of God's glory being revealed on the earth. Even the darkest and most troubling events of history serve that end. His sovereign governing hand will take the divergent streams of human events and draw them together so that they issue into the ocean of his own glory. Listen to Jonathan Edwards writing in *A History of Redemption*:

> God's providence may not unfitly be compared to a large and long river, having innumerable branches, beginning in different regions, and at a great distance one from another, and all conspiring to one common issue. After their diverse and apparent contrary courses, they all collect together, the nearer they come to their common end, and at length discharge themselves at one mouth into the same ocean.

But what about the streams that seem to be heading in the wrong direction, away from the sea rather than toward it? Edwards has an answer:

> The different streams of this river are apt to appear like mere confusion to us, because we cannot see the whole at once. A man who sees but one or two streams at a time, cannot tell what their course tends to. Their course seems very crooked, and different streams seem to run for a while different and contrary ways: and if we view things at a distance, there seem to be innumerable obstacles and impediments in the way, as rocks and mountains, and the like; to hinder their ever uniting, and coming to the ocean; but yet if we trace them, they all unite at last, all come to the same issue, disgorging themselves in one into the same great ocean. Not one of all the streams shall fail.[4]

I like that last expression: "Not one of all the streams shall fail." Such is the power of God in governing the world that not only do all things happen by his power, but they will all be made to serve his purposes. The governance of providence thus underscores once again the trinitarian nature and purpose of reality. The Trinity does everything as an act of God-centered love. That is what it means to say that God is love—the

Father and the Son and the Spirit live to honor, exalt and enjoy one another in the works of creation, providence, judgment, and redemption.

Fourth, providence affirms that *God cares and provides*. If governance points to God's purpose in history, sustenance points to God's involvement in history. He upholds and empowers all things. Berkhof defines God's providential sustenance as "that continuous work of God by which he maintains the things which he created, together with the properties and powers with which he endowed them."[5] This act of sustenance can also be called preservation. Donald Guthrie summarizes the detailed way in which God preserves and sustains his creation:

> In the teaching of Jesus, there is a specific emphasis on God's special care for his creatures. To show the detailed nature of God's providential care, he states that not even a sparrow, which men rank as little, falls to the ground apart from the Father's will (Mt 10:29). This is further substantiated by the view that the heavenly Father feeds the birds, without their having to sow, reap or store their food (Mt 6:26ff.). . . . Even more significant is his knowledge of the hairs of the head, which vividly demonstrates his interest in the minutest details of human life (Mt 10:30). Moreover, sun and rain are under his control and operate irrespective of the worthiness of the recipients (Mt 5:45).[6]

If the image suggested by God's governing of the cosmos is God as King, then his sustenance of the cosmos points to God as Father. Thus the idea of sustenance points both to the love of God for the work of his hands ("he doesn't make junk and he doesn't junk what he has made") and to the absolute dependence of everything upon God's care and sustenance.

Finally, providence is consistent with the notion that *God uses means*. Some theologians speak of a third element in the doctrine of providence. They identify this third element as concurrence. This may be defined as "the cooperation of the divine power with all subordinate powers, according to the pre-established laws of their operation, causing them to act and to act precisely as they do."[7] Another way of putting this is to say that God governs and sustains everything in creation and culture through secondary causes and not outside of them. Thus while God sustains the life of the sparrow, he does so normally through the food chain. Although he is responsible for the rise and fall of nations, he uses social, economic, political, and military factors to bring about his intended ends.

Two questions come to mind. The first has to do with miracles. The second has to do with human freedom and responsibility. We begin with miracles.

If God exercises his providential control over the cosmos through secondary causes, then what place is there for miracles? If God uses medical doctors to heal sick people, then what do we do with miraculous healing? If God does use miracles, is concurrence a real part of providence?

Miracles do not pose problems to providence if the relationship is rightly understood. Although God uses the laws of nature usually in ruling and sustaining his creation, he is free as a sovereign ruler to change his habits. Charles Kingsley's statement is apt: "There are no laws of nature, only habits of God." Miracles do not violate the so-called laws of nature which God normally uses in the concurrent rule of his cosmos. Miracles, therefore, are the exceptional actions of God. He, more than anyone, has the right and freedom to act exceptionally.

What about human freedom? The parable teaches that human freedom is not contradicted by God's sovereign rule ("if God caused it then I wasn't meaningfully involved") but that, conversely, God's sovereign rule is the *condition* of human freedom ("God's sovereignty makes it possible for me to make decisions and take action"). This view that divine determinism and human freedom are complementary truths is known as *compatibilism.* This view teaches that in order for an act to be free and responsible it has to come from the heart, that is, it has to be something one really wants. The old way of looking at human freedom stressed the importance of neutrality ("I am free to choose any of several options equally"). What the old view failed to deal with adequately is the fact that intensity of desire and not variety of choices is the crucial element of a decision.

Let me illustrate this by thinking back on my courtship with my wife Lois. I was deeply in love with Lois (and still am, I might add) and wanted very much to marry her. Now suppose that a good friend came up to me and said, "Mark, your decision to marry Lois will not be a free and responsible decision until you check out the other women on campus and consider marrying them." This might sound like wise advice. But the point of dating other women would not be to make a decision based on neutrality (i.e., "I am equally open to marrying Lois or Mary") but simply to sort out what the true desires of my heart were. If Lois was the woman I loved, no number of choices of other women that did not include Lois would have made my decision free. And if marrying Lois was what I really wanted, then even if she were the only choice, the decision would have been a free and responsible one. My point then is that "freedom" in a decision involves doing what you really want more than it involves having a number of choices. The choices serve a deeper purpose. They help us to determine our heart's desire and thereby move us toward a truly free decision of doing or choosing what we really want.

What all this means for the doctrine of providence is that God may be behind my every decision, but as long as I am doing what I really want to do I am exercising my free will and my decisions are worthy of praise or blame.

Two biblical arguments support this understanding of human freedom. One is Acts 2:23, 36: "This man [Jesus] was handed over to you by God's set purpose and foreknowledge; and you, with the help of wicked men, put him to death by nailing him to the cross. . . . God has made this Jesus, whom you crucified, both Lord and Christ." Note two things here. First, God providentially was behind the crucifixion of Christ. God purposed that Christ should die. Second, men and women who wanted him dead are still held responsible for the action. Why? Because they were doing what they wanted. Although their actions were foreordained, they were acting on the basis of the desire of their hearts to get rid of the religious troublemaker from Galilee once and for all. They were free and responsible because they did what they wanted. God was acting sovereignly in foreordaining the action. Both God's actions and the actions of humans were free because they were from the heart: God's heart to save sinners and humankind's heart to get rid of God.

The second biblical argument for this new view of freedom comes from the passages that praise God for his actions. How can God be praised for doing good when he has no real choice (that is, from the old way of looking at freedom)? God doesn't have a real choice between committing sin and doing good. God is "locked in" to doing good. Only if freedom means the liberty of doing what is in our hearts can we regard God's actions as "responsible" and "free." We would argue that this view of freedom applies to human actions as well. Thus, divine determinism and human freedom are seen as compatible. When God acts concurrently in history with the actions of human beings, both are free even though the latter's actions are determined by God's will.

But what does this say about God's relationship with the evil done in history? It seems Huck had a question about that as well. Let's turn to it.

God Hates Sin and Suffering but Uses It for His Glory

No feature of the doctrine of God's providence has aroused more controversy than the problem of evil. If God controls everything that happens, and evil happens, then God is responsible for evil. God's defense, the case made by his creatures on his behalf, is called a *theodicy*—justifying God against the charge that he cannot be both good and omnipotent and thus has wronged humankind. Let me offer four perspectives on God and his relationship with evil and suffering.

First, "evil is inherent in the risky business of free will" (J. B. Phillips). While we must reject a humanistic understanding of free will, we can strongly affirm an Augustinian understanding of free will. People must be held responsible for doing what they want. God never wants to do evil. He has no evil desires in his heart and, therefore, cannot pass on evil desires to anyone. He cannot be held responsible for either the origin of evil or the continuance of it. People who are doing what they want to do, should they choose evil, must be regarded as responsible.

This does not mean that social, political and economic forces do not influence individual behavior. The person who lives in a Brazilian *favela* may turn to petty thievery more readily than a wealthy landowner living on a successful plantation in the country. But the desires of the heart of our slum-dweller belong to him. Let's say that the *favela* dweller not only feels compelled by social and economic conditions to steal, but that he loves the act and feel of stealing. He loves the pain that it inflicts on others. He loves the act of breaking the law. Just as it would be wrong to blame him for the social conditions and forces beyond his control, it would be wrong to absolve him from whatever evil is in his heart. He has free will, and evil is inherent in that risky business.

God's relationship to this sinful action of humankind can be called judgment through privation. Undeniably, God has a right to judge sin.

But how does he do so? Romans 1:24 speaks of God giving people up to their sin. The theological term for this is *privation*. When God judges sin in this way, the result is not testimony against God's goodness, but rather for it. When God withdraws his presence, the sunlight of holiness and righteousness disappears and the shadows of evil and sin predominate. This says to me that God is light (that is to say, holy and without sin or evil in himself except as things that he hates) and therefore cannot "create" sin or evil. He can only withdraw from it, thus deepening the darkness of the sin or evil. Thomas Watson described the process of privation as "a withdrawal of influence":

> God does not infuse evil into men, he withdraws the influence of his graces, and then the heart hardens of itself; even as the light being withdrawn, darkness presently follows in the air; but it were absurd to say, that therefore the light darkens the air; and therefore you will observe, that Pharaoh is said to harden his own heart. . . . God is the cause of no man's sin. It is true God has a hand in the action where sin is, but no hand in the sin of the action.[8]

One way to think of this is to imagine a concert pianist playing on a piano that is horribly out of tune. She has a right to play the piano as a concert pianist. She has the expertise needed. She is playing all the right notes. Yet her playing has a discordant sound which she herself dislikes, although the "fault" of the sour notes is in the piano and not in the pianist. A casual observer might mistakenly accuse the pianist of playing off key, but the observer would be wrong. The pianist was doing the right thing (playing all the right notes). The piano must bear the blame. Thus when God gives up men and women to their sin (Rom 1:24), he is playing the right notes in the lives of his creatures by separating from their sin. The evil within their hearts is the cause of their discordant behavior.

A second proposition is that some suffering can have beneficial purposes and outcomes. Certainly the world of medicine offers examples of this. The pain of chemotherapy for the cancer patient is purchasing perhaps years of additional life. But in a deeper sense suffering can make us more human, can sensitize us to the plight of others, can free us from the "dark little dungeon of our own ego."

A third proposition is that much suffering and evil is caused by Satan and merely permitted by God. Job 1:6-12 clearly teaches that the real author of evil is Satan. A whole range of evils from the deaths of children to disease and economic disaster are linked to Satan's direct attempts to destroy Job's faith. But Satan's power is limited (because he is a creature), and therefore he cannot operate without God's permission. God finds Satan's actions abhorrent and yet permits Satan to act, knowing that he can bring good even out of the evil that his enemy will do. God then should not be blamed for the natural disasters and evils of life. Satan is the more probable source of such things. God acts in our lives to overrule the acts of the enemy.

A fourth proposition is that the cross vindicates the God who suffers with us. The parable ends with Twain's wife defending the reality of his suffering and laying to rest Huck's doubts about his goodness. Is this going too far? Can God suffer? How does this square with what was said in an earlier chapter about God's impassibility?

Evangelical theologians have been willing to talk of the suffering of God even while affirming the truth of his impassibility (the idea that God does not have fits of emotions or moods as do we creatures). Luther spoke of the "crucified God." Contemporary evangelicals proclaim that "God himself is the great sufferer and has fully met the problem of evil in giving his own Son, Jesus Christ, at infinite cost to himself."[9] Millard Erickson writes that "God is a fellow sufferer with us of the evil in this world. . . . God himself became the victim of evil so that he and we might be victors over evil."[10] John Stott affirms that "if God's full and final self-revelation was given in Jesus . . . then his feelings and sufferings are an authentic reflection of the feelings and sufferings of God himself."[11] How do these theologians come to make these statements and still hold to the impassibility of God?

I find John Stott's discussion in *The Cross of Christ* very helpful. He explores the issues of the suffering of God and the impassibility of God in light of the cross. Let me summarize his discussion.

First of all, Stott recognizes the importance of the doctrine of God's impassibility. While he is unhappy with how uncritically the early fathers borrowed the notion of *apatheia* or impassibility from Greek philosophy and applied it to God, he admits that they were safeguarding an important biblical truth about God's transcendence:

They were wanting above all to safeguard the truths that God is perfect (so that nothing can add to or subtract from him) and that God is changeless (so that nothing can disturb him). We today should wish to maintain these truths. God cannot be influenced against his will from either outside or inside. He is never the unwilling victim either of actions which affect him from without or of emotions which upset him from within. As William Temple put it, there is a highly technical sense in which God, as Christ revealed him, is 'without passions'; for he is Creator and supreme . . . free from gusts of feeling carrying him this way and that.[12]

Stott then points out the biblical case for acknowledging the reality of God's feelings in general and his suffering in particular. Jeremiah 31 and Isaiah 49 represent a host of chapters that describe the vigor of God's feelings for Israel: "I have loved you with an everlasting love. . . . Can a mother forget the baby at her breast? . . . Though she may forget, I will not forget you! . . . all my compassion is aroused." The feelings of compassion are coupled with feelings of grief and pain. Judges 10:16 speaks of how God can "bear Israel's misery no longer," implying that he fully shared in their feelings of suffering. Genesis 6:6 boldly declares that "the LORD was grieved that he had made man on the earth, and his heart was filled with pain." Although admitting that the language is anthropomorphic, we must still affirm that some real truth about God's heart is being revealed and that something akin to what we call pain is part of God's inner life and nature. Abraham Heschel, in his book *The Prophets,* goes as far as to say that "the most exalted idea applied to God [in the prophets] is not infinite wisdom, infinite power, but infinite concern."[13] Jeremiah 31:20, which in the Hebrew speaks of God's bowels being troubled by Ephraim, testifies to the reality of pain in God over human sin and suffering. First Corinthians 1:25, which speaks of the foolishness and weakness of God, is relevant here.

Stott concludes his discussion of God's suffering revealed in Christ and its value for theodicy by quoting a playlet called "The Long Silence." The setting is God's throne room, and the masses of the earth's people stand before God to be judged. But righteous indignation seizes several in the crowd; they feel that God has no right to judge them, for he cannot know how they suffered; instead, he should be judged for the evil he did to them. A Jewish victim of a Nazi concentration camp reveals her hideous tattooed camp number. A black man shows the rope burns around his neck from the lynching that he suffered just for being black. A pregnant schoolgirl shares the wounds of shame and public disgrace. Thousands more join in the protest against God. All those who feel that they are more victims of sin than sinners decide to judge God rather than be judged by him. They pronounce their sentence on God:

Let him be born a Jew. Let the legitimacy of his birth be doubted. Give him a work so difficult that even his family will think him out of his mind when he tries to do it. Let him be betrayed by his closest friends. Let him face false charges, be tried by a prejudiced jury and convicted by a cowardly judge. Let him be tortured.

At last, let him see what it means to be terribly alone. Then let him die. Let him die so that there can be no doubt that he died. Let there be a great host of witnesses to verify it. . . .

And when the last had finished pronouncing sentence, there was a long silence. No-one uttered another word. No-one moved. For suddenly all knew that God had already served his sentence.[14]

To understand God's relationship to evil and suffering, we must see him first as one who feels pain keenly, one who suffers deeply and eternally in a way appropriate to a sovereign God. Through the actions of his providence, God expresses and redeems that pain through Christ. The problem of suffering is solved only by the worship of a crucified God.

The Truth of God's Providence Can Increase Our Glad Dependence on God

The story ends by Twain's revealing what all the twists and turns of the story ultimately mean. Life is but the story of coming home to God: "You and Jim are now part of our real family." Here are words of joy and comfort. A skillful author has guided his beloved characters to safe harbor and a new future. The joy of Huck and Jim will overflow once the truth of what is happening begins to sink in. What about us? Does providence fuel our joy in God? I am convinced that it can. Take the following six comforts that the truth of God's providence can give to us.

God is in control. When Christ spoke of God's care of the sparrow (Mt 10:29), he spoke of the comforts of God's providential care for us. "God's providence gives us a security in this insecure, often violent world," writes Bruce Milne. "The Lord sits enthroned over all the military, political, social, and economic forces of our generation and his eternal predetermined purposes are ripening through it all."[15] In light of the fact that our whole lives are in the hands of a great and good God whose heart for us has been revealed in Christ, we can live with a joy that circumstances and troubles cannot kill. Milne puts it well: "We can therefore live day by day knowing that the hands which hold our lives are the same hands which hold all things."[16]

Christ and his cross will be exalted. The most startling act of providence is mentioned in Acts 4:27-28:

> Indeed Herod and Pontius Pilate met together with the Gentiles and the people of Israel in this city to conspire against your holy servant Jesus, whom you anointed. They did what your power and will had decided beforehand should happen.

Jonathan Edwards, writing in his *History of Redemption,* reflects on the meaning of the cross for all of history. He concludes that it is the focal point of providence:

> God created the world to provide a spouse and a kingdom for his Son: and the setting up of the Kingdom of Christ, and the whole spiritual marriage of the spouse to him, is what the whole creation labors and travails to bring to pass. This work of redemption is so much the greatest of all the works of God, that all other works are to be looked upon either as parts of it, or appendages to it, or are some way reducible to it. . . . And we need not wonder that so much is made of it in Scripture, that it is so much insisted on in the histories, and the prophecies, and songs of the Bible; for the great work of redemption is the subject of the whole, its doctrines, its promises, its types, its songs, its histories, and its prophecies.[17]

The cross makes possible the salvation of rebels, who now constitute this new kingdom of redemption. All the lines of providence flow into and out of Golgotha. The death of Jesus Christ is the answer to the puzzle of history.

God will preserve his church. When I am tempted to get discouraged by the way the church fails, God's providential control of all things seen through the lens of the cross restores my hope. The Westminster Confession of Faith speaks of how providence "taketh care of his church, and disposeth all things to the good thereof" (chapter 5, section 7). Robert Shaw, commenting on this section of the Confession, was moved by the promise to God's people implicit in the doctrine of providence:

> The preservation of the Church, in spite of the craft and malice of hell, and of all the pernicious errors and bloody persecutions which have threatened her ruin, is no less wonderful than the spectacle which Moses beheld—a *bush burning* but not *consumed*. And let us still confide and rejoice in the promise of Christ, that the gates of hell shall never prevail against the church.[18]

This does not mean that we can neglect the reform of the church through our Spirit-directed labors. Rather, the doctrine of concurrence teaches that God will use us to preserve and protect and even perfect his bride.

Suffering can be redemptive. By this I mean that God can bring good out of evil. He can strengthen our love and delight in him and mortify our sins and unbelief through the mystery of providence working through suffering. When Sarah Edwards heard of her husband's death by an inoculation for smallpox, she found her soul strengthened in faith and love for God and not embittered. She wrote to her daughter on receiving the news:

> What shall I say? A holy and good God has covered us with a dark cloud. O that we may kiss the rod, and lay our hands on our mouths! The Lord has done it. He has made me adore his goodness, that we had him so long. But my God lives; and he has my heart. O what a legacy my husband, and your father, has left us! We are all given to God; and there I am, and love to be.[19]

Sarah's comment brings to my mind a statement of Cotton Mather on the death of his child: "May the death of my children be the death of my sin." An awareness that God governs all things for his glory and the good of his people, bringing them into glad dependence on him, has led many of his saints to deepen their delight in him and see him for the treasure that he is, even in hours of grief and loss.

Prayer becomes essential. Knowing that God is the Creator and I am his creature, that he is the author and I am a character, may seem to reduce me to helpless passivity. In fact it should lead to a strong emphasis on prayer. The author of reality has disclosed to me that he writes his story in dialogue with his characters. Prayer represents one of the most powerful and free acts that I can do. Knowing that my freedom consists in doing what I want, and yet knowing that God has ordained everything (even the desires of my heart), I might feel trapped. Yet he has revealed to me that I can cry out for a clean heart (Ps 51:10; Heb 8:10). He can give me the holy desires that will give me the freedom to live in the joy of the Lord. Prayer thus becomes the most powerful and free act that a creature/character can engage in. God, who appoints all ends, has appointed all means to reach those ends. Prayer is one of those appointed means. He will accomplish his ends through the prayers of his people. We have not, because we ask not.

We don't need all the answers if we have Christ. This may not satisfy many people, but it gets at an important point. I do not know specifically why God works the way he does in his providence or how he will glorify himself through the deaths in Bangladesh or the ovens of Auschwitz. Yet Christ has spoken to the troubled Philips of this world: "Anyone who has seen me has seen the Father" (Jn 14:9). I cannot see the blueprints of God's secret decree, but I can see Christ, and in him I see the Father's rainbow of grace and blessing arching over my turbulent world.

Conclusion
Submitting to the truths of providence can break the fever of fitful doubt and fill me with the enjoyment of God. When I am tempted to ask "why," I need to hear Paul's admonition in Romans 9:20 to be silent before God's providence (what right does the clay have to challenge the potter?) not as an outrage to my humanity, but as the humble silence which turns to glad submission.

Take heart and comfort from Psalm 91:1-2: "He who dwells in the shelter of the Most High will rest in the shadow of the Almighty. I will say of the Lord, 'He is my refuge and my fortress, my God in whom I trust.' "

Questions for Individuals or for Group Discussion

Part One
1. The parable stresses that the distinction between God and humankind is like that of an author and his characters. What are your thoughts

on the value of such an analogy?

In what ways does the analogy work?

What are some limitations of the analogy?

2. How does the parable deal with the problem of evil?

How is the author-character distinction used to resolve the problem of evil?

3. Why does Huck react with anger when Twain reveals that he is the author?

How is that anger resolved?

Why would it help him if he knew Twain's heart?

4. What does this parable reveal about the Trinity and its role in history and providence?

5. Is Twain's death in the story real? Explain.

Is the suffering real? Explain.

How can an author suffer on two levels?

6. What is the meaning of the scene at the wharf?

Does the end of history have a role to play in theodicy (the justifying of God)? Explain.

7. In what ways could this parable help you resolve some of the tensions in the sovereignty-versus-freedom debate?

In what ways is the parable not of much help?

Part Two

8. The plan or decree of God logically precedes the doctrine of providence. The Westminster Confession of Faith defines this decree as follows: "God, from all eternity, did, by the most wise and holy counsel of his own will, freely and unchangeably ordain whatsoever comes to pass." What is the biblical support for such a definition?

What is the relation of the plan to providence?

9. List the three parts of the doctrine of providence. What Scriptures support these three aspects of providence?

10. The first part of providence is governance. The "Theology Behind the Story" section states that God's purpose in governing history is to express his joy and love for each of the persons within the triune family. What evidence is given for this view?

What would you add to or change about the argument?

11. How is the notion that God's sovereign providence is compatible with human freedom explained?

Which evidence is the most convincing to you?

Which arguments are the least satisfactory?

12. What objections must theodicy overcome?

What does the idea of privation teach?

Do you think it helps or hinders in understanding God's relationship to sin and evil?

13. Do you agree that the problem of suffering is solved only by the worship of a suffering Savior? Explain.

Does the doctrine of God's impassibility contradict the idea that God suffers? Explain.

14. What are some of the main benefits of the doctrine of providence?

Which benefits mean the most to you?

How can it increase your joy in God?

For Further Reading

For a searching study of the subject of providence and its spiritual value for the believer, one could do no better than to read John Flavel's *Mystery of Providence* (Carlisle, Penn.: Banner of Truth Trust, 1964; first published in 1678). Based on Psalm 57:2, the study centers on the conviction that "a great part of the pleasure and delight of the Christian life is made out of the observations of providence." This work may also be found in volume 4 of Flavel's *Complete Works,* also published by the Banner of Truth. A pastoral and biblically based discussion of the problem of evil can be found in D. A. Carson's *How Long, O Lord* (Grand Rapids: Baker, 1990).

Chapter Seven
Humanity and Sin:
Ratty, Mole
and the Magic Flute

P*lease answer the question,"* the judge (none other than the Owl) said sternly to the defendant shifting uncomfortably on the witness stand.

"I will repeat the question," said the distinguished prosecuting attorney, one Mr. Weasel, Esq. "Did you not willfully and with malice aforethought brutally murder the god Pan on Willow Island under cover of darkness three nights ago from this very evening?"

"Objection! Objection!" screamed Toad, Ratty's lawyer. "I don't give a hoot how distinguished Mr. Weasel may be, he is badgering the defendant!"

"Objection overruled," shouted the judge, casting an angry glance at Toad and turning to the Water Rat. "You will answer the question or be held in contempt of this court. And mind your references to 'hoots,' Counsel."

Ratty scanned the courtroom. His eyes met those of Mole, who lowered his head and turned away. There was nothing else to do but confess everything, starting right from the beginning of that fateful day. The courtroom was mesmerized as Ratty narrated the following story:

Life by the river on this July day was as rich and full as ever. Cattails waved in the hot breeze. Sunlight slid over the surface of the river like paint over a canvas. The grassy banks were filled with play and laughter and picnic baskets brimming with melons and meats. Reeds swayed like island dancers to a music none could hear but all could see and feel. Ratty smiled upon this idyllic scene. He was waiting for his good friend Mole. Together they would do some exploring down the river, drifting in Ratty's small water craft with the current, following the river wherever it might lead. He fussed about getting things packed while he waited, and was careful to place his new carving knife in the billowing baskets of food.

Mole arrived in due course, looking nervous but excited at the same time. Mole relied upon Ratty's bravery and expertise in most things, and although Ratty knew this, he never belittled his dependent friend for it. "Shall we be gone long?" asked Mole.

"We shall drift downriver till dark, then paddle our way home by moonlight," Ratty said with delight and adventure dancing in his eyes. "Shall we go?" And with that question he scooped up picnic baskets and paddles and filled the midsection of their boat with the abundance. Mole gingerly put one foot into the boat and then stood inert, one foot on board, the other on shore.

"Do get in," said Ratty with a mixture of good humor and mock irritation. Then, with a yank of his friend's paw, he pulled the reluctant Mole into the boat and stuffed a pickle in his mouth before he could complain.

With a push of the pole the boat was away from the bank and out in the swift current. The two great friends, their paws dangling in the cool water, were being carried off to adventure and into the unknown.

After several miles of drifting downstream, Ratty suggested that it was time for lunch. Mole agreed. Within minutes of this motion and its second, Ratty and Mole were munching with delight on the cakes and melons and cold meats that made up their picnic feast. Mole was humming to himself and watching the waves of heat sway upon the horizon of the field in which they were picnicking. Ratty was quite busy, however, rummaging around in the seemingly bottomless basket for something. With a cry of delight he emerged from among the melon rinds and boiled eggs, holding a book.

Mole caught the title just before Ratty flipped the book open and riffled through its pages. He thought the title read *The Quest for Pan,* but he was not sure. Suddenly Ratty whooped. "There he is," Ratty said breathlessly, "Pan— god of Nature."

"I've never heard of him," admitted Mole. "What is he like?"

"Mysterious," said Ratty, continuing to turn the pages of his book, searching for more information about Pan. "He's never been seen, but we all owe him quite a lot," Ratty said to the incredulous Mole, who found it hard to take in new information with his mouth closed.

"With his flute he plays the music that creates and sustains the world of the river. The swaying willows, the moist banks, the flowing river, and we animals that live along the river—all of us are products of the inaudible song of Pan that floats in the air night and day."

"Do you mean that you and I are no more important to him than the insects that swirl about the marsh, that we are all equally the products of Pan's music?" Mole asked with great concern. He swatted one of those upstart insects, which had landed on his cheek as he spoke.

"No, not exactly," said Ratty after a thoughtful pause. "We, the animals that talk, are not only created by Pan, but created in his image." Ratty smiled, being quite pleased that he had been able so easily to handle Mole's difficult question.

"And what does it mean to say that we—talking moles and mice and such—are in the image of Pan?" Mole asked.

"Well . . . let me think for a moment," said Ratty as he assumed a thinking position, elbow and arm propping up head, and picnic basket propping up elbow and arm. After a few moments, during which Mole consumed that last piece of strawberry pie, Ratty gave another one of his hoots that signaled some satisfying discovery.

"Think of the 'image of Pan' like this," explained Ratty. "We possess the powers to join in the music-making with Pan. We can see the musical score as if it were all around us. The visible world is but the staff and notes of his composition. But we, as thinking and talking animals, are aware of that while the other creatures along the river bank aren't."

Mole had to think that one over. Ratty caught his breath and plunged on. "Furthermore, we are like Pan in that we are partners with him in shaping life along the river. We need him to give us life and strength, and so we are in a relationship of loving dependence on him and are used by him, with our full consent, in building the web of life along the river (the food chains, carrying on the species, and things like that)."

Mole looked puzzled. "Do you mean, Ratty, that Pan's music, which I can't even hear, has made me and shaped me into a mole who enjoys digging holes and eating and boating with his friends along the river?"

"That's it!" Ratty shouted.

"What's 'it'?" Mole shouted.

"That's really what makes us like Pan—we seek our joy in the things we do. That's the way Pan does everything. He is seeking to celebrate his life as god by making music, and so he makes creatures like us who seek our joy both in working and playing along the river and in seeking Pan. Pan lives to enjoy his music, and he creates image-bearers like us who live to enjoy both the music-maker and the things that his music makes."

"Are we seeking Pan?" asked Mole with some surprise.

"I didn't tell you that before, but that is why we are heading downriver today. By tonight, if I have read the map in this book, *Quest for Pan*, correctly, we will arrive at Willow Island, where Pan has been sighted in the past."

Mole nodded with a mixture of exhilaration and terror at the prospect of actually seeing Pan, the awesome god of nature. That thought also made him hungry, and he poked his head back into the basket.

Hours later the light began to fade. Mole had curled up in the bottom of the boat for a little nap. Ratty gazed up to watch the night sky being born. The stars appeared one by one against the black backdrop of night. The moon was soon riding along with them downriver, stroking the water with its beams.

At the very moment that moonlight and starlight and night breeze met, the music began. In the gathering darkness the Rat could see the outline of the island ahead. Ratty grabbed his book and began to read the chapter on Willow Island and the appearances of Pan. His eye caught a heading in the chapter entitled "The Coming of Noise." As the music grew louder, his eyes scanned the page and what it said about the noise:

The creation of the world of the river took place (we are told by popular legend) on Willow Island. Pan began to play the music that brought the beauty of the river world into existence. One of the creatures, however, whom legend identifies as a crow, at the time the sweetest singer of all the bird world, desired to possess the music solely for himself and sought to steal Pan's magic flute. The crow fought fiercely for the flute but was unable to wrest it from the god. As he flew away in defeat, Pan cursed him. Ever after, the crow would be unable to sing, but would only make a harsh noise. This harsh noise possessed a dark power, for it would undermine the music of Pan's flute that serenely filled the river world. The noise would create in the unsuspecting hearer a deep hatred for the river world, one's fellow animals, oneself, and ultimately for Pan and his music. Thus legend teaches that the music and the noise are in ongoing conflict, and each creature along the river is under this curse.

Ratty closed the book. The beauty of the music had grown now and was filling his soul with moonlight and waterfalls and the brightness of the stars. His love and joy in Pan and in the river grew with every strain of the music. His whole being leaned toward the shore of the island. Soon the boat was gliding through the reeds and slid up onto the island's grassy banks. What was this nonsense about a curse!

At that moment two things happened. The first was that Mole woke up, rubbed his eyes and asked where they were. The second was that Ratty could no longer hear the music but was instead filled with the discordant caws of a flock of angry crows. The noise pounded at his brain. He began to feel that it was all Mole's fault and commenced screaming at his totally bewildered friend. He would have choked him on the spot if Mole had not jumped over the side of the boat into the cold water. The puzzled Mole scrambled up the banks of the island and hid in the bushes, shivering from cold and fright.

Ratty reached into the picnic basket and grabbed his knife. He staggered from the boat and made his way to the center of the island, at times hearing the music of the flute, at times the noise of the crows. Both were growing louder as he entered the clearing and saw Pan. Ratty's eyes were wide with wonder and fear.

Pan was standing with his back to Ratty. He was all circled in golden light, and his whole body swayed back and forth to the music of his flute. He turned his head to reveal his profile. His face was filled with an expression of delight.

Ratty moved stealthily along the ground, cloaked by the shadows. *It must be Pan who is the source of the noise that is beating against my brain,* thought Ratty. His knife glistened in the moonlight. Saliva began to drip from his mouth. In an instant Ratty was upon the god, stabbing and gnawing and ripping with fierce intensity. Blood and hair were everywhere. Within minutes it was over and there was only silence.

Ratty looked around in horror at what he had done. He threw the knife down to the ground and ran back to the boat, calling for Mole as he went. Mole said nothing, but silently and efficiently fetched the knife and the flute from the clearing. He concealed them under his vest and returned to the boat.

The two did not speak to each other either on the return voyage or when they parted for their homes in the early hours of morning. The next day Ratty was arrested for the murder of Pan and now found himself on trial.

"So you now confess to this brutal murder which you previously denied?" asked the prosecuting attorney.

"Yes, I confess," said Ratty, to Toad's shock and to the prosecutor's delight.

The jury recessed, deliberated for about fifteen minutes, and then returned with the verdict of guilty. The Owl sentenced Ratty to ten years of wandering along the river in order to experience the fullness of the curse of noise and then to be put to death. The judge also expressed appreciation on behalf of the court for Mole's cooperation with the prosecution and particularly for providing the knife and the flute that sealed Ratty's fate. Mole lowered his head in humility. A dejected Rat was then taken away by the constable, and the courtroom emptied.

Mole walked slowly back to his hole. He had heard the music that night at the island, although he never admitted it to Ratty or to anyone else. He said nothing about the music because he might then have to tell about the noise and how it drove him to pick up the knife after Ratty had dropped it; drove him to strike the final blow at the still breathing Pan; drove him to conspire against his former friend. "Well done, well done," the voices of the crows seemed to be saying. Mole held his head in pain. He hoped that this would pass and that life along the river would return to normal. He had his doubts.

The Theology Behind the Story: Humanity and Sin

The quiet, breezy world of the river is disturbed forever by the crimes of Ratty and Mole. The god Pan is murdered, and his creatures did the deed. The parable raises questions about who we are as creatures and what is wrong with our world. These are the very questions addressed by one of the worldview convictions stated in chapter one:

> What's wrong with me and my world? I am headed in the right direction when I affirm in heart and mind that the human creature has rebelled against the triune God's purpose for human life (God-centered culture building) and that this rebellion is cosmic in scope, extending to humanity's being, society and culture, history and religion. The primary expression of this rebellion is idolatry. Because of this rebellion and idolatry, suffering, evil, and death have been unleashed into human experience. The goodness of creation and culture has been horribly misdirected, being used now for idols rather than for God.

The parable tries to catch a glimpse of the terrible truth that humanity in particular and creation in general have been horribly marred by sin and its curse. We want to look at three central ideas in the remainder of the chapter.

Remember: the aim of our pilgrimage is to increase our joy in God. Knowing the sobering truth of sin seems to lead in the other direction. It doesn't have to. Even the savage truths of sin can increase our joy in God. How? Consider the suggestion of the Heidelberg Catechism. Question four asks how many things we need to know in order to live and to die in the comfort that we belong to Christ. The answer is "Three. First, the greatness of my sin and their wretchedness. Second, how I am freed from all my sins and their wretched consequences. Third, what gratitude I owe to God for such redemption."[1]

Strangely enough, my enjoyment of God can be fueled by a sense of the "greatness of my sin and wretchedness." The reason that joy rather than depression results from such knowledge is that Christ's work in setting me free "from all my sins and their wretched consequences" produces a profound gratitude "for such redemption." This is evangelical logic at its best. We travel with Ratty and Mole to the island; we let our heads throb with the shrill noise of sin and rebellion; we sit through the condemnation of the God-killers in the courtroom—all so that we may know our own wretchedness as sinners and Christ's excellence as Redeemer. We turn to that subject in our next chapter. But for now we must return to the scene of the crime.

The Bible Presents the Human Creature as Bearing the Image of God

In the parable Mole was curious about the animals' relationship to Pan—god of nature. Ratty's thoughtful reply was quite a discovery for Mole:

"We, the animals that talk, are actually created not only by Pan, but created in his image." Ratty smiled, being quite pleased that he had been able so easily to handle Mole's difficult question.

But Mole wanted to know more about what it meant to be in the creator's image. So do I. A number of answers have been given to that important question of the *imago Dei*. The phrase *image of God* comes from the classic text in Genesis 1:26-27:

Then God said, "Let us make man in our image, in our likeness, and let them rule over the fish of the sea and the birds of the air, over the livestock, over all the earth, and over all the creatures that move along the ground."

So God created man in his own image, in the image of God he created him; male and female he created them.

Interesting phrase, this "image of God." I'll mention three views (out of many possibilities) that have tried to explain just what the image is all about.

First, *the image as qualities from God.* In the parable, Ratty suggests that the image of God refers to our higher, rational powers, to be "thinking and talking animals." This is sometimes known as the essential or substantive view of the *imago Dei.* This view hears Genesis 1:26-27 saying that the image refers to something the man and woman *are.*[2] Such a view holds that the image is not lost by the fall into sin. Genesis 9:6

(where the image is referred to) is sometimes used in support of this.

Second, *the image as dominion from God.* Ratty felt more was involved in being in the image of the creator than just the possession of certain qualities. He gropes to explain something deeper about the image: "Furthermore, we are like Pan in that we are partners with him in shaping life along the river." This is known as the dominion or functional view of the image. For Ratty the functional view of the image involves being Pan's partner in creation. Those in the real world who are attracted to this view point, for support, to Psalm 8:5-6: "You made him a little lower than the heavenly beings and crowned him with glory and honor. . . . you put everything under his feet." The psalmist is referring back to Genesis 1:26-27. He seems to have the idea of "image" in mind when he mentions that man and woman are made a "little lower than the heavenly beings." And, just as in Genesis 1, the concept of rule and dominion is spoken of in connection with the image. "Then God said, "Let us make man in our image, in our likeness, and let them rule"(Gen 1:26).

Third, *the image as relationship with God.* Ratty doesn't say much about a third understanding of the image of God that could be dubbed the relational view, but this view is a significant interpretation of the *imago Dei* for some theologians. A good statement of the relational view is given by Leslie Stevenson in his *Seven Theories of Human Nature.* In setting off the Christian view from all others, Stevenson points to the Christian understanding of image as relational.

> The most crucial point in the Christian understanding of human nature is the notion of freedom, the ability to love, which is the image of God himself. . . . The attainment of the true purpose of human life—love of God, and life according to his will—is open to all.[3]

This view bears a closer look. I am taken with the idea that we reflect the Trinity in its mutual love and interdependence. God is ultimately relational, living to honor and exalt and serve one another within the Trinity. We were made to enjoy and serve others for God's sake, just as God has done.

Is it true to say that being in God's image means living to enjoy God and his works? That may sound soft and flabby for a theological definition. I think it has some muscle, however. Consider the following three conclusions:

The image involves essential, functional, and relational elements. Each of the three views of the image mentioned above has merit. I agree with the substantive view that human creatures, like God, are rational and that this separates us from the animal world. I agree with the functional view that humanity, like God, is a culture builder and hence has the power of dominion over the creation. I agree with the relational view that human beings, like God, are most fully human when they are loving God and others, expressing the I-thou character of their essential makeup. But simply to say that all three are correct is not enough. I do believe that one of the views towers above the others: the third view.

The image means that the human creature, like God, is personal. "Essentially . . . we are like God in that we are persons."[4] God is personal. What does that mean? God is relational. He is Trinity, existing eternally in one indivisible nature expressed through three persons who live to exalt, enjoy, and serve the other members of the divine family. Ranald Macaulay and Jerram Barrs, in their book *Being Human,* elaborate on the personal and relational nature of both God and humanity:

> Like God, we relate to everything personally—he is creative and so are we: we are given dominion over the earth—a dominion intended originally to be benign and so to reflect God's own dominion. We are also made for personal relationships—man with woman, woman with woman, man with man and both with God. These relationships are to be characterized by love in the same way that the relationship among the members of the Trinity is a relationship of love.[5]

Macaulay and Barrs stress, then, the personal and relational character of both God and his image as the key to solving the enigma of humanity. Human creatures are relational, made to love God and others.

The image consists in loving God and others. All of this leads Macaulay and Barrs to a stunning conclusion. In light of the fact that humans, like God, are personal, they are to live in relationships of God-centered love and joy.

Therefore, Jesus' summary of the Law and the Prophets, that we are to love God and our neighbor, can be viewed as a clarification of the phrase "image of God" in Genesis 1. The image loves because love is of God (1 John 4:7). And the image's purpose is to love. Here is a definition of what it is to be human.[6]

The great commandment is a definition of what it means to be in the image of God. What a statement! To keep God's law of love is to be fully human, to fully image God and his relational nature. Listen again to the words of the great commandment as it is recorded in Mark 12:29-31. A teacher of the law has come to Christ with a burning question: "Of all the commandments, which is the most important?" Christ is not caught off guard by this, because he knows that God is love and hence what the creature must do and be to properly "image" God's essential being:

> "The most important one," answered Jesus, "is this: 'Hear, O Israel, the Lord our God, the Lord is one. Love the Lord your God with all your heart and with all your soul and with all your mind and with all your strength.' The second is this: 'Love your neighbor as yourself.' There is no commandment greater than these."

To bear the image means loving God and others just as the Trinity does: living to enjoy, honor, and serve God and his creatures with our whole being. Notice how Ephesians 5:1-2 supports this understanding of the image: "Be imitators of God, therefore, as dearly loved children and live a life of love, just as Christ loved us and gave himself up for us as a fragrant offering and sacrifice to God." To image God is to live a life of love. What kind of love? This love is not some sort of vague humanistic love, but a radically God-centered love, a love that is just like Christ's.

How does this relational view deal with the valid insights of the substantial view and the dominion view of the image of God? This law of love (which is the image of God) is expressed through culture building as I seek to glorify and enjoy God through glad dependence and seek to meet the needs of others through work and service. Qualities of rationality and creativity make possible the imaging of God through God-centered love, for these are the powers that are used to love God and others. Thus the truths of the substantive view and the dominion view are served.

But does this definition of the image of God as the law of love apply to fallen humankind—who do not love God fully and the neighbor unselfishly? Genesis 9:6 makes it clear that the image of God is still there in fallen humanity. We would furthermore say that the law of love cannot be eradicated without eradicating the creature. Part of the goodness of creation is that God has built his law into everything, but only in the man and the woman does the highest expression of his law of love unfold.

That goodness of creation law cannot be extinguished; it can only be misdirected. Thus Paul in Romans 2:15 teaches that the Gentiles have the law of love written on their hearts and hence will be judged on this basis. The woman and the man can live in open contradiction to their image, to the law of love, but they cannot destroy the fact that every fiber of their being encodes this law.

Does the image of God involve our bodies in any way, or is it just a law in our souls? Here again we must avoid dualism. To do this we need to digress for a moment and talk about the constitution of humankind. Only then can we talk about the degree to which our bodies are in the image of God.

I reject the traditional dichotomous (we are body and soul) or trichotomous (we are body, soul and spirit) discussions of the constitution of humanity, for I fear that dualism clings to them. I would recommend Millard Erickson's position of "conditional unity" as an improvement over traditional dichotomous or trichotomous views. This view teaches that the human creature is a unity of immaterial and material qualities. "The spiritual and the physical elements are not always distinguishable, for man is a unitary subject; there is no struggle between his material and immaterial nature."[7] This view emphasizes that man is a unity and not a duality (in a Platonic sense) of a spirit imprisoned in a body.

But doesn't such a view play into the hands of secularists and other reductionists who have been "monists" all along, insisting that humanity is just material? What happens at death? If the body disintegrates, do we simply cease to be? Although the normal state of the human is to exist as a unity of body and spirit, this unity can be broken at death and the two elements separated. This is only a temporary separation, however, as 1 Corinthians 15 teaches, for there will be a time of resurrection in which body and soul will be reunited.

How does this view of the human constitution answer the question about whether our material bodies are part of the image? If God is spirit, how can our physical bodies reflect him? The answer is that my body is the embodiment of the law of love. My brain, my hands, my sexuality— all are ways of living a life of love. My body is a necessary part of the image of God, not because God has a body, but because his law of love in a material world is meaningless if I cannot obey it with hands and feet, brain and brawn. Nothing about me is irrelevant to the law of love. The law of love is encoded in tissue and cells and muscles and corpuscles as well as in spirit and mind. My whole being is the tablet on which is written the law of God. I am in the image of God body and soul.

But something terrible has happened to the image.

The Heart of Sin Is Aversion to God

The closer Ratty and Mole got to Willow Island, the stronger the music of joy became. Much to their surprise, the music was up against some deafening competition. The noise became stronger than the music and transformed them in strange and disturbing ways. Ratty's journey of worship became a tragedy of blood lust as he attacked Pan. But Ratty was not alone in the crime of "theocide." At the end of the parable Mole's secret sins and his own troubled conscience are revealed to the reader.

Mole's accusing thoughts tell us several things about sin. Sin began through actions in history. At heart, sin is an incurable allergy to God. It is a perversion of the image of God that constitutes us. This allergy is made up of the elements of pride, lust, and unbelief. This allergy has been transmitted to all of Adam's posterity. The curse of this allergy touches all of life and all of creation. These statements need some elaboration.

The beginning of sin: the historic Fall. The parable speaks of a fall that took place in the world of the river when the crow sought to steal Pan's magic flute. The parable describes the result:

Ever after, the crow would be unable to sing, but would only make a harsh noise. This harsh noise possessed a dark power, for it would undermine the music of Pan's flute that serenely filled the river world. The noise would create in the unsuspecting hearer a deep hatred for the river world, one's fellow animals, oneself, and ultimately for Pan and his music.

What is the biblical parallel of this event? Listen to Moses' description of the coming of the noise in Genesis 3. We see the serpent tempting Eve to eat the forbidden fruit, telling her that she not only would live (even though she disobeyed God) but would live a fuller life with her eyes "open." Eve does listen and wrestles in her conscience. Here's what happens next:

When the woman saw that the fruit of the tree was good for food and pleasing to the eye, and also desirable for gaining wisdom, she took some and ate it. She also gave some to her husband, who was with her, and he ate it. Then the eyes of both of them were opened, and they realized they were naked; so they sewed fig leaves together and made coverings for themselves. Then the man and his wife heard the sound of the LORD God as he was walking in the garden in the cool of the day, and they hid from the LORD among the trees of the garden. (Gen 3:6-8)

What monumental verses! The whole creation is shaken forever by the events recorded in these three verses. We need to look at both the nature and the implications of this fall into sin.

The heart of sin: the allergy to God and reactionary idolatry. The Fall narrative tells us that Adam and Eve disobeyed God. This was the substance of their sin. But the passage also gives us a couple of indicators as to the heart of the sin that was committed. First, Genesis 3:6 lists the reason Eve disobeyed. The account says that Eve saw the food was "good," "pleasing," and "desirable." In other words, Eve wanted the benefits of the fruit more than she wanted to be true to God. Being image-bearers impels us to desire God, because he is the object of the love and longing of our hearts, minds, souls, and bodies. But Eve distorted the image. The power to love and desire God was now redirected from God toward something that God created. In other words, the heart of sin is idolatry—loving and desiring the creation more than the Creator.

Second, when the fallen couple heard God in the garden, they hid. Not only did they direct their whole humanity to loving and desiring something else besides God, but they now had an aversion or allergy to God. Not only is he no longer the supreme treasure and delight of their lives; he now is undesirable, unattractive and even repellent to fallen humankind. The words of Romans 8:7-8 come to mind: "The sinful mind is hostile to God. It does not submit to God's law, nor can it do so. Those controlled by the sinful nature cannot please God."

The heart of sin is that God is now an object of hostility and his will an object of contempt and rebellion. Just as the law of love makes God the object of love, so sin makes God the object of hate. Sin's new law is to invert the Great Commandment so that it now reads: "The Lord your God is now repellent. Hate the Lord your God with all your heart and mind, soul and strength. Treat your neighbor, who bears the image of God, accordingly." We can call the heart of sin an allergy to God. He literally makes us sick. Berkhof describes this horrible truth:

> Now there is no doubt about it that the great central demand of the law is love to God. And if moral goodness consists in love to God, then moral evil must consist in the opposite. It is separation from God, opposition to God, hatred of God, and this manifests itself in constant transgression of the law of God in thought, word, and deed.[8]

This antipathy for God and penchant for God-substitutes is called idolatry—the love of anything else more than we love God (cf. the first commandment). This sin is the cause of the wrath of God described in Romans 1:18 and following verses. It is clear from that passage that idolatry is rampant in human culture and that it is the heart and root of all other sins.

Some of the biblical words for sin confirm this understanding. *Hamartia* is the most common word for sin in the New Testament, used, along with other members of this word-family, over three hundred times. It is also the word used to translate the Hebrew word *hāṭā'* (found over two hundred times in the Old Testament). The basic meaning of *hamartia* is "missing the mark." This sounds innocent enough. Perhaps we picture the athlete trying with all her might to set the record, vault over the cross-bar, or break the tape at the end of a race. Perhaps she misses the mark. We still may feel that she gave her best effort. This is the wrong idea. *Hamartia* refers to intentionally failing to reach the goal or hit the target. To stay with the athletic image, *hamartia* refers to the athlete who takes money to blow the game or throw the match. It involves willful moral failure. A good example of the use of *hamartia* is Romans 3:23: "For all have sinned and fall short of the glory of God." Sin is failure to see God for who he is and delight in and treasure him with one's whole being. John Piper explains:

> Make no mistake, sin is diametrically opposed to the glory of God. Romans 3:23 says that sin is a "falling short" of God's glory. . . . Paul means that sinners have fallen short of *prizing* the glory of God. We have exchanged the glory of God for something else: for images of glory, like a new home or car or VCR or computers or vacation days or impressive resumes or whatever makes our ticker

tick more than the wonder of God's glory.[9]

What is the mark that we were made to attain, the goal that we were empowered by our good Creator to reach? The Great Commandment contains the goal: "Love the Lord your God, with all your heart, all your mind, all your soul and all your strength" and "love your neighbor as yourself." Sin is the inversion of this commandment. It is the treasuring of anything else more than we treasure God. That is the mark that is missed.

A second biblical word for sin is *asebeia,* which carries the meaning of "godlessness" or "impiety." It is the negative of *eusebeō* (to worship) and *eusebeia* (piety or godliness). The word is used in Romans 1:18: "The wrath of God is being revealed from heaven against all the godlessness *[asebeian]* and wickedness of men who suppress the truth by their wickedness." What is the godlessness mentioned in this verse? Verses 21 and 23 explain that it is an allergy to God that breaks out into idolatry. "For although they knew God, they neither glorified him as God nor gave thanks to him, but their thinking became futile . . . and [they] exchanged the glory of the immortal God for images." Sin is godlessness—the refusal to worship and delight in God as one's highest treasure and, in turn, to treasure and delight in something other than God as the highest good or greatest joy. Thus refusal to enjoy God supremely is at the heart of the biblical understanding of sin. This second biblical word supports the truth pointed to by *hamartia.* Sin is an allergy to God.

But what about the bad things we do to one another? Doesn't this emphasis on the God-centeredness of sin fail to explain the more common occurrence of sinning against another human being? I don't think so. The sins against our neighbors—the innocent irritations, the cranky cruelties, the words of slander or accusation, the cold shoulder, the secret pleasure at another's failure or pain, the indifference to someone's need—have deeper roots than just the current heat wave or noisy kids or the capitalist system. I have a floating hatred of and aversion to God buried deeply in my unconscious that tends to surface over time when I see the reflection of God's face too clearly in another human being. We strike at the image of God before us in flesh and blood, hoping in our heart of hearts to hurt the reality that stands behind the image.

The elements of the allergy to God: pride, lust, and unbelief. The dynamics of idolatry are many, but three elements seem to be at the heart of this allergy to God: pride, lust and unbelief. We saw this above when we mentioned Romans 1:18-23. Paul spoke of these three elements of pride (the refusal to glorify or give thanks to God), lust ("God gave them over to their desires"), and unbelief (their minds became futile and darkened). Two additional passages support this anatomy of sin. First John 2:16 mentions two of these three elements in an attempt to summarize the rebellious world-system that denies God and his claim to be glorified. "For everything in the world—the cravings of sinful man, the lust of his eyes and the boasting of what he has and does—comes not from the Father but from the world." Pride and lust have a major part in the ecology of the fallen world. But there is a third part to the ecology. Hebrews 3:12 contains the warning "see to it . . . that none of you has a sinful, unbelieving heart that turns away from the living God." This unbelief would seem to be logically prior to either pride or lust, for the rejection of God's truth-claims is logically prior to believing in something else and treasuring it as a substitute for God. I want to look more closely at these three things.

Pride is the most prominent element of sin. This does not mean that pride acts with outward arrogance all the time. Pride can speak softly, but the message is always the same: I do not need God. Pride is a sin against the first commandment, for it involves putting the self (or family or nation, etc.) in the place of God. Martin Luther declared that human pride "is only concerned with itself, seeks only its own advantage, and always ignores anything that might get in its way. It even passes over God himself as though it did not even see him and is completely self-centered."[10] Does this mean that fallen humankind is irreligious? Not at all. This pride can express itself through religion. We can even "exploit" God for our own ends.[11] Spiritual pride is particularly odious to God, as the story of the Pharisee and the publican illustrates (Lk 18:9-14).

Lust is the second element of idolatry. We take God's good gifts of a relationship with himself, ourselves, our neighbor, and all creation and culture and use them with ingratitude. We are like spoiled children at the supper table, our plates heaped with good things. We refuse to eat what we are given and fuss and whine for something else. We do this to strike at God, to hurt him if we can. So we prefer to grab what we want when we want it rather than pray and wait for God's good gifts in his time. We prefer the fevers of lust and unbridled appetite to the pleasures of enjoying God and his generous nature.

Notice what pride, lust, and unbelief do to our essential nature as God's prophet, priest, and king. As prophet, each is to interpret the world for God, loving God with the whole mind. As priest, each is to worship and delight in God above all other things in life. This is the religious task of humankind and speaks of loving God with all our hearts. As king, each is to rule the world for God, building God-centered cultures. This is the cultural task of loving God with all our strength.

Pride is the inversion of our kingly task. Instead of ruling the world for God, I now want to use everything in culture and creation as though I were the center of the universe. Lust is the inversion of our priestly task. Instead of leading creation in the enjoyment of God, I want to regard anything and everything else as more pleasurable and delightful than God. Unbelief is the inversion of our prophetic task. Instead of interpreting the world in a God-centered way, I will offer virtually any other kind of interpretation of reality so long as it pushes God to the periphery. I will accept scientific interpretations, philosophical interpretations, psychosexual interpretations, even religious interpretations. The one requirement is that I do not posit the triune God of the Bible as the heart of reality. What a complete reversal of our original purpose for being!

All of the above discussion about this allergy to God has begged one question. How did this allergy get passed down from Adam to us?

The transmission of the allergy to God: guilt, corruption and condemnation in Adam. The Bible makes it clear that sin is passed on to the descendants of Adam and Eve. David lamented that he was "sinful at birth, sinful from the time my mother conceived me" (Ps 51:5). We know from Genesis 3 that Adam and Eve were cursed because of their sin and that the curse of sin stains every life that follows; nevertheless, some questions arise. How did this disease of sin, seen so clearly in Genesis 3, get passed on to David and all the rest of us? Is it fair for God to hold us responsible for what somebody else has done?

These questions lead us to the topic of original sin. One would think that original sin meant *the* original sin, that is, the sin that Adam and Eve committed. This is not the case anymore. The term has come to mean the sin that we begin life with. Inherited sin might be a better term for this, but we won't mess with tradition on this point.[12]

The classic text on the transmission of sin is Romans 5:12-21. Let me quote the relevant portions of that passage:

> Therefore, just as sin entered the world through one man, and death through sin, and in this way death came to all men, because all sinned. . . . For if, by the trespass of the one man, death reigned through that one man, how much more will those who receive God's abundant provision of grace and of the gift of righteousness reign in life through the one man, Jesus Christ. Consequently, just as the result of one trespass was condemnation for all men, so also the result of one act of righteousness was justification that brings life for all men.

Paul seems to be teaching that Adam's sin has affected us all. "By the trespass of the one man, death reigned." Furthermore, this condemnation of all in Adam leads to death for all. The stickiest point is in verse 12. Paul states that death came through one man's sin and yet we all die because "all sinned." Does this mean that sin and death were introduced by Adam and these blights were passed on when we followed Adam's bad example and committed actual sins? This is an unlikely explanation for two reasons. First is that the stress on Adam as representing all humankind is overpowering ("by the trespass of the one man"). Simply seeing Adam as a bad example does not do justice to the force of these words. Second is the parallel with Christ. Christ saves me by my union with him, not just by setting a good example. I inherit eternal life on the basis of his works, not my own. So too with Adam. I am in union with Adam and inherit the consequence of his alienating works. How then did I sin in Adam?

I have found the view known as *federalism* to make the best sense of the passage. This view teaches that Adam and Christ are representative heads of the human race. This means that they do not act merely as private persons, but on behalf of the mass of humankind. All those in Adam are held responsible for what their representative did. He sinned, became guilty, experienced a corrupted nature, was condemned, and died. I, therefore, inherit the guilt, corruption, and condemnation by merely being human and having Adam as my federal or covenantal head. The parallel with Christ I find clinches the argument for me. He is my representative before God and wins for his posterity deliverance from guilt, corruption, and condemnation. I receive this good inheritance from Christ not because I have earned or deserved it because of my personal actions, but because I am in union with the Redeemer. My experience of sin and death is the shadow side of this truth. I am in Adam. Through that cursed union I die. Through union with Christ I live.[13]

The cosmic scope of the allergy to God: total depravity and the curse of death. What is the scope of sin? We need to mention a few things about total depravity and the comprehensive influence of sin on all of life.

The depth and breadth of sin are given a chilling description in Romans 3:10-20. Paul strings together a host of Old Testament references to make the point that humanity is totally unable to save itself, because it has been morally disabled by the depravity of sin:

> There is no one righteous, not even one; there is no one who understands, no one who seeks God. All have turned away, they have together become worthless; there is no one who does good, not even one . . . so that every mouth may be silenced and the whole world held accountable to God. Therefore no one will be declared righteous in his sight by observing the law; rather, through the law we become conscious of sin.

Sin is both universal and total. Everyone in the world without exception is under the curse of sin. Thus, it is universal. But each person has been corrupted by sin in every area of life: one's will (Rom 7:14-24); one's heart and desires (Mk 7:21; Rom 1:24-27; Eph 2:3); one's understanding (Eph 4:18); and the whole of one's behavior (Gal 5:19-21). *Total depravity* is the term for the truth that sin touches every area of our life. We do not do anything out of a pure and passionate love for God as our highest joy. We must pray with Augustine that God forgive us of even our best deeds. This does not mean that we are as bad as we could be. Those who are outside of Christ enjoy God's common grace which restrains (but does not eradicate) the evil that they do.[14]

Note also that sin rips all of life down the middle. Here we must watch out for the ghost of dualism. The Fall means that "the whole creation has been groaning as in the pains of childbirth right up to the present time" (Rom 8:22). We see the distortion of sin in our personal lives. "Murder, adultery, theft, blasphemy, and many other vices are obvious and wide-spread infringements on God's creational design for human life."[15]

Nature has been touched as well, for even the ground has been cursed because of human sin (Gen 3:17). Cultural life has been affected. In the academic sphere we see sin distorting the quality of thinking, teaching, study and the relationships among students, faculty, and administration. In the arts we see bad taste, the obsession with distorted sex and gratuitous violence. Like the rippled mirrors at the amusement park, everywhere we look we see only distorted images of what was meant to be.

The Bible has a word for the whole network of distortions that pervade every area of life. It is called the *world*. We are exhorted in Romans 12:2, "Do not to conform any longer to the pattern of this world." Herman Ridderbos, in his study of Paul's theology, attempted to define what Paul meant by "the world." His conclusion was that the world consists of "the totality of unredeemed life dominated by sin outside of Christ."[16] Satan is at work distorting each and every area of life so that the glory and beauty of God cannot be seen in it. It is as a usurper and vandal of God's good creation that Christ referred to Satan in John 12:31 as "the prince of this world." This world (seen as a good creation) does not belong to him but to God. The "world" (seen as the sum total of all of life dominated by sin) does belong to Satan and will be destroyed by God.

We must be clear to distinguish, then, two possible meanings of "the world." It can refer to the totality of creation and culture as God sees it and is therefore good. It can refer, by contrast, to the totality of life under sin and evil. What the Bible does not mean by "the world" is that area of life we tend to refer to as "secular." Worldliness can creep into prayer as much as politics, into preaching as much as playing sports.

How can I hold that creation and culture are still good although they are, at the same time, dominated by sin and, therefore, part of the fallen world? How can I read a novel or befriend my non-Christian neighbor and be in the world but not of it? The key is to think in terms of *structure* and *direction*. Structure is the creational goodness that God builds into everything. Everything has an inextinguishable goodness by virtue of its having been made by God and for his glory. The origin of creation and culture and the ends of creation and culture do not change. God's goodness and glory dominate each. What then constitutes worldliness? Worldliness has to do with direction. *Direction* refers to the religious use that is made of creational life. Is it being used for God or for idols? Is my work in the office for God or for idols? Is my hymn-singing directed toward God or toward idols? Is my ownership of houses and lands for God or for idols? Everything is structurally good but directionally a battleground.

Thus sin and its curse are comprehensive in scope. The Fall affects everything without exception. The dust of death has settled on all of life. Alienation now fills the cosmos. We are alienated from God, others, ourselves, as well as from creation and culture. We need to look more closely at these effects of sin.

The Curse of Sin Is Massive Alienation

The parable opens with an ugly courtroom scene. The prosecuting attorney has Ratty on trial for murder and hurls a sharp and damning question at the accused: "Did you not willfully and with malice afore-thought brutally murder the god Pan on Willow Island under cover of darkness three nights ago from this very evening?" Ratty is convicted of the crime largely from evidence given by his former friend, Mole. The circles of alienation that ripple from the crime of theocide move farther and farther outward, turning friends into enemies and idyllic river life into a dark scene of death and violence.

In general usage *alienation* refers to the experience of being a stranger, estranged from others, from the world around us, from God, from ourselves. The Bible uses the term in several places (Gal 4:17; 5:4; Eph 2:12; 4:18; Col 1:21), but even more widespread than the term itself is the theme of alienation. This theme runs through the Scripture. It refers, in a comprehensive way, to the effect of sin on our lives. Before we were redeemed by Christ, we were never quite at peace in relationship with God, in our family life, on the job, with friends, in church, with the creation, or with ourselves. We always felt something was missing. That feeling is the feeling of alienation.

Consider first the fact of *alienation from God*. We can talk about four ways we experience alienation in our relationship with God (and there are probably others). (1) Alienation from God's presence. The man and the woman were expelled from the garden because of sin. Made for fellowship and the enjoyment of God, humankind is now alienated from the relationship that meets this deeply rooted need. In our fallen state we are under God's wrath. (2) *Alienation from God's will.* Romans 8:7 describes the sinful bent of our will, which "is hostile to God" and "does not submit to God's law, nor can it do so." Our will is free only to choose that which displeases God, whether we are making choices in a church, a shopping mall, our offices or our homes. (3) *Alienation from God's word.* We become deaf to the word of God in creation and deaf to the word of God in Christ and in the Scripture. It does not make sense to us outside of Christ, and we hear it preached as a strange and alien message. (4) *Alienation from God's Gospel.* Sin produces pride. We pretend that we don't need God. When we ponder God's existence and what we owe him as our Creator, we determine that we can justify ourselves before him with our moral, religious, or cultural achievements. Legalism (as practiced by Pharisees in the Gospels and Judaizers in Galatians) is one such manifestation of self-justification.

Consider, second, the fact of *alienation from others.* Take note of the faces of alienation in our relationship with others. Sin produces a *spirit of enmity* between people. Rivalry, racism, social divisions, class conflicts, divorce and church divisions are but some of the faces of estrangement behind our conflicts. Sin produces *exploitation* of our neighbor. *Fear of others* is another face of alienation and sin. We are afraid that our neighbor will find out the truth about us, that we are full of anxiety and dread and self-loathing, and will misuse that information, condemning us or treating us as inferior. We hide from our neighbor behind elaborate defense mechanisms and masks. We seek to communicate, even in the midst of alienation, and sense the deep misunderstanding, guardedness, and insularity that keep us from hearing one another in a deep and compassionate way.

Consider, third, the fact of *alienation from ourselves.* Sin brings the *loss of meaning and purpose.* This is one of the most characteristic effects of sin and one of the most chronic maladies of alienated humankind. The book of Ecclesiastes chronicles the struggle of a sage with the emptiness of life in a fallen world. Sin also brings *self-deception.* Romans 7:23 describes the plight of the alienated person (Paul using himself as an example) as he seeks self-understanding: "But I see another law at work in the members of my body, waging war against the law of my mind. . . . What a wretched man I am! Who will rescue me from this body of death?"

Consider, fourth, the fact of *alienation from creation and culture*. The manifestations of alienation in my relationship with creation and culture would include the *exploitation and destruction of our environment.* Humanity does not see nature as the psalmist did, declaring the glories of God. Humanity reduces nature to a supermarket of raw materials to be consumed in response to human schemes and desires. Alienation also shows itself in *cultural fatigue and world-weariness.* John Cheever, the novelist, has written that the main emotion of North American adults, with all their advantages of wealth and education, is disappointment.[17]

Such is the bitter inventory of sin's effects. When we do not treasure God supremely as our greatest delight, the enjoyment of everything else in life slowly drains away.

Conclusion

With the help of Ratty and Mole we have explored the dark world of fallen humanity. Several affirmations were made: namely, that the Bible defines man and woman to be in the image of God, that the heart of sin is aversion to God, and that the effect of sin is massive alienation.

In light of the parable and the comment, we turn again to the worldview question, "What's wrong with me and my world?" This question has a distinctive answer for a Christian:

What's wrong with me and my world? I am headed in the right direction when I affirm in heart and mind that the human creature has rebelled against the triune God's purpose for human life (God-centered culture building) and that this rebellion is cosmic in scope, extending to humanity's being, society and culture, history and religion. The primary expression of this rebellion is idolatry. Because of this rebellion and idolatry, suffering, evil, and death have been unleashed into human experience. The goodness of creation and culture has been horribly misdirected, being used now for idols rather than for God.

The curse is cosmic in its scope. I am helpless to free myself from the distorting grip of sin and its curse. But even while I spiritually wriggle on my back like a helpless insect, someone has taken compassion on me. Someone has entered my insect world to restore my true humanity. To that grand restoration of troubled insects we shall turn in the next chapter.

Questions for Individuals or for Group Discussion

Part One

1. How does Ratty explain the meaning of the image?

What biblical support does his view have?

How significant is the element of joy in defining our humanity and our image-bearing?

2. What is the music, and what role does it play in the story?

What does it correspond to in reality?

3. How is the Fall explained in this story? Compare and contrast with the biblical doctrine of the Fall.

According to the parable, how does the Fall affect our image?

4. According to this parable, what is original sin?

Are the traditional explanations of pride, lust, and unbelief dealt with in this parable?

5. How does the parable deal with the results of sin?

What is the impact of sin our relationship with God, the creation, and others?

Are the elements of sin and guilt brought out sufficiently in the story?

How is alienation pictured in this parable?

6. Compare Ratty's depravity with Mole's.

7. What biblical evidence do we have that theocide is inherent in total depravity?

What light does the crucifixion of Christ shed on this question of hating God (cf. Acts 2:36-37)?

What remnants of sin remain in the believer?

Does this allergy to God remain? Support your answers from Scripture.

8. What should be our response in ministry and in our personal lives to the presence and power of sin?

Part Two

9. The idea of the image of God in humanity is presented as relational in character. What does this mean?

What biblical support is there for this view?

Does it take account of the valid insights of the other views?

10. Define original sin.

How does the federal view explain the transference of guilt, condemnation, and corruption from Adam to his descendants?

What is the biblical support for this?

11. What is meant by the definition of sin as "aversion to God"?

What is the evidence in the Scriptures that might support such a view?

12. How is worldliness defined in the comment section?

Does this definition avoid dualism? How?

13. The comment section presents alienation as massive—that is, a moral and religious plague that has touched all of life in its totality. What is the biblical support for this view?

What examples of this kind of alienation come to your mind?

For Further Reading

On the subject of humanity, I would recommend Ranald Macaulay and Jerram Barrs, *Being Human: the Nature of Spiritual Experience* (Downers Grove, Ill.: IVP, 1978). On sin and grace one would benefit from Thomas Boston's *Human Nature in Its Fourfold State* (London: Banner of Truth Trust, 1964; orig. 1720). Ever timely are Ralph Venning's *The Plague of Plagues* (London: Banner of Truth Trust, 1965; orig. 1669) and J. I. Packer's *Knowing Man* (Westchester, Ill.: Crossway Books, 1979).

Chapter Eight
Redemption:
The Insect

I *woke up Monday morning* in my parents' Soweto home only to discover that I had become an insect.

I had been a flesh and blood human being when I went to bed. Now, although I remained in my own room, I had changed. I was covered with numerous legs. Where my face should be I had a hideous pair of eyes, pincers, and long antennae which moved about in front of me like nervous fingers tapping the arm of a chair. I had gone to sleep as an African youth of eighteen on Sunday night, having stumbled home drunk, raging at my parents for their angry words and nagging manner. I had woken up on Monday morning an insect with no face.

I lied to my mother when she knocked on the door of my room at seven a.m. and asked whether I was all right. I told her I was sick and could not go to work. The door was locked so that she could not enter. I heard her call my father. I scurried into the corner, trying to hide in the shadows. My father knocked. He told me to unlock the door. I told him that I was too sick to get off the bed. I saw his eye wandering about in the keyhole, searching the room. He began to shout that I was lying, that he could see my bed and I was not there. Then he stopped shouting. He saw me. He saw my bloated, black, crusted body. He saw my half-dozen legs. He saw my scissorlike mouth. He saw me through the keyhole and screamed.

I heard footsteps running back to the kitchen. I heard the phone being dialed and terrified gasps and my mother's screams and sobs. I moved out from the corner and closer to the door to hear the conversation. They were talking to my uncle, who was regarded by all as a holy man in Soweto with special connections with God. Uncle was also a big shot in politics. He was in the royal line of the Besotho people and had inherited much of the ancestral lands back in Lesotho, but had come to live in Soweto, God knows why. Then I heard them hang up. My mother's screaming continued in the kitchen. I hated her for screaming. I hated my father for calling my uncle. I had, in fact, hated them as long as I could remember.

My father returned to my door and demanded to know who I was and what I had done to his son. I explained that I was his son but that I had woken up as an insect. He left the door again and paced the house, yelling to Mulungu, the god of earth and sky.

When my uncle arrived, he came to the door and talked to me. What had happened? he asked. I loved my uncle but I did not trust him, for, after all, he was my father's brother and with what good could my father ever be associated? I repeated my story. There was silence. He asked me whether I was hungry. I told him I was hungry. He placed plates of food in front of the door and then went back into the kitchen. I unlocked the door with some difficulty and then slid the plates into the room and closed and locked the door again. I ate savagely.

For the next two days (Tuesday and Wednesday) this routine was repeated ten or twelve times. I would talk with my uncle, whose words comforted me, and then he would leave me food. My parents kept away completely, probably in the kitchen.

On Thursday, I could hear the three of them having an argument. My father was yelling that I must be reported to the authorities, that this was intolerable, that he would lose his own job as a houseboy if he called in sick one more day. My uncle agreed that he should go to work on Friday but that he must tell no one about the situation. My mother continued to scream and sob. I felt itchy, and my room was filled with putrid odors.

Friday morning my father went off to work. My uncle told my mother to sleep, for she had been up all night, praying and sobbing. Uncle spoke to me all that day. He told me about his memories of my birth. He was the one, he reminded me, who had given me my first soccer ball and had coached me on my first team, the Spirit of Biko. He had gone with me to job interviews when I had dropped out of school and had helped me land my job as a clerk at a government office in Johannesburg. He had been saddened, he said, by the rage he saw building within me, rage about apartheid, my parents, my limited future, my life. I hardly listened, thinking only of the next plates of food that would be brought to me, and growing impatient with the delay.

It grew dark at 6:30. My father was late, and I could tell that my uncle was worried about something. In the distance, coming down the dirt street that our house was on, I heard a crowd of people moving in the dark. Out of my window I could see torches and staves. Someone was carrying a tire. I could see my father at the front of the crowd. I could hear them yelling in my tribal tongue.

My uncle went to the door as the mob surrounded the door. I heard my father's voice. He told my mother and uncle to come out, for they were going to burn the house. My uncle told my mother to do as my father said. She gathered a few things and joined the crowd outside the house, her face shiny with tears.

My uncle refused to leave the house. He said that he would not let me be burned to death. My father yelled back that his son was already dead, that the insect had eaten him and that some magic had given the insect power to mimic his son's voice. My uncle told the crowd that there was no evil magic at work except the power of hate. I had become an insect because I was consumed by hate. I would become a man again if the power of hate was broken. The righteous anger of the high God against hate itself had created two insects, Uncle said. One was me, the other was this mob. The mob shouted my uncle down, and someone threw a rock that cut my uncle's forehead and made it bleed. He picked up the stone, gripped it in his fist and, after staring into the mob, went back into the house.

I was sure that they would torch the house within seconds, but they hesitated, perhaps wondering what my uncle would do next. Then the crowd began chanting for my uncle to send me out. They would spare the house. They just wanted me destroyed. They called for me, but I did not move. I was frozen in terror.

I looked out the keyhole of my door and saw my uncle stretched out on the floor, head buried in the carpet, tears flowing freely, talking as though to some unseen person. As I watched, something happened to my uncle. A great foul odor filled the house, and I saw his face disappear and legs begin to wriggle from every part of his swelling body. He had become an insect. I could not look any longer, and I backed away. I heard his many legs shuffling toward the front door.

In an instant he had rushed through the door into the crowd. Fire was thrown on him, and one of his legs burst into flame. Men were on him, pulling the tire over his body. He was now on his back in the middle of the dark street, stars above him like the eyes of a thousand insects watching the fate of one of their own played out before them. Uncle was covered with petrol and set on fire. He screamed in anguish as his brittle body crackled and curled with the burning. The mob watched in silence as the insect died. They had finished the work they came to do. They went to their homes in fearful quiet as the smoke circled above them and wretched odors engulfed them. The insect burned through the night.

By dawn, the dirt street was littered with windswept ash.

My parents would not come into the house, fearing the curse of whatever spell was on it. They stayed with neighbors all day Saturday.

I slept off and on throughout Saturday, finally waking in the deep darkness of Sunday morning. I was hungry but could only think about my uncle's death. I opened the door of my room and looked around. The house was dark and quiet. I opened the front door and crawled slowly into the street. My eyes darted in every direction to be sure no one was watching. I stood in the midst of the smoldering ash. *These ashes should have been mine,* I thought. *I am the insect that should have died.* I rolled my bloated body in the ashes and cried for revenge against my father, against my neighbors, against God. I knew that my cries would arouse the neighbors and I would be discovered. The ashes that I had stirred swirled about me and filled my eyes and throat and stuck to my legs. They irritated my eyes to the point of tears and filled my throat until my enraged cries were choked into silence. The ashes refused to assist my hatred. By choking my screams they had silenced my shouts of malice. I felt a crack in the depths of my ugliness. Something had broken in the hidden labyrinths of an insect heart.

I opened my eyes and looked around. Instead of antennae, I saw my fingers. Instead of insect legs, I saw the legs of a human. My hand moved to where my face had once been. I felt lips and eyes and a human nose. I jumped up, still covered with ash, and ran toward the house to look in a mirror.

I stopped suddenly in the open doorway. My uncle was standing in the living room grinning at me. I could hear movement in the street behind me but could not turn, could not take my eyes off my dead uncle who was now alive in front of me. He looked unscathed from the abuse he took two nights before except for the cut on his forehead from the stone. He reminded me of the words that he had uttered days before. Hate makes insects out of people. God gives them up to that change so they can have their wish to devour all around them. Their punishment is to become what their hatred wants them to become. But when the power of hate is broken, the power to be human returns. He then pointed behind me and told me that our work was now just beginning, that we would have to gather up the ashes, would have to feed our neighbors and care for them, and would have to repeat the story of the last few days to them so that they would become well. He held out the stone to me. I took it and clutched it tightly in my hand.

I turned around and looked out into the street. It was filled with human-sized insects, old and young, their discarded torches of the night before lying by their bloated bodies. We immediately gathered plates of food, mingled with ashes, and began to work for the coming metamorphosis.

The Theology Behind the Story: Redemption

How would you feel if you awoke one morning and discovered that you were an insect? Not the best way to begin the day. But imagine your relief when you were made right again—restored to full humanity. In this section we will look at how God restores us to true humanity after the ravages of sin have made us buglike in soul and heart.

In the worldview affirmation of the first chapter, we saw that the renewal of everything depends on Christ. Herman Bavinck defined the redemptive heart of the Christian faith as follows: "God the Father has reconciled His created but fallen world through the death of His Son, and renews it into a Kingdom of God by his Spirit."[1] The parable wrestles with these themes. I would like to highlight five points the parable makes about salvation.

Salvation Is the Restoration of—Not Escape from—Creation
One of the most striking things about the parable is the way everyone gives up on the young man turned insect—everyone, that is, except the uncle. The uncle had loved him before his repulsive transformation. "He told me about his memories of my birth. . . . He had gone with me to job interviews when I had dropped out of school and had helped me land my job as a clerk." The uncle also had watched with great sadness as the young man filled with a growing rage—a rage that eventually dehumanized him. But the uncle not only refuses to give up on the young man, or on the rage and hate that fills Soweto, but also gives his life over to restore the young man and his whole world.

In this way the parable teaches that salvation is not just "going to heaven," but rather restoring God-centered living on earth. As Albert Wolters says, "God doesn't make junk and he doesn't junk what he has made." To demonstrate that this is a biblical way of thinking, I offer three arguments for the idea that salvation means the restoration of creation.

1. Many of the key words for salvation are translated with the prefix *re-*, indicating that salvation is a restoring of creation and not an escape from it. Consider the word *renewal* (*anakainōsis,* used twice in the New

Testament). This is used in Romans 12:2 for the "renewing of your mind." Sanctification, a stage in salvation, is pictured not as an escape from thinking but as a return to correct, God-centered thinking. Regeneration (*palingenesia*, used twice in the New Testament) is used in Titus 3:5: "He saved us through the washing of rebirth and renewal by the Holy Spirit." The picture here is of salvation by the Spirit, not as giving up on humanity but as offering a radical new start from within. It is the making new again of something old. The only other occurrence of this word is in Matthew 19:28: "Jesus said to them, 'I tell you the truth, at the renewal of all things, when the Son of Man sits on his glorious throne, you who have followed me will also sit on twelve thrones, judging the twelve tribes of Israel.' " This is an even more dramatic support of salvation as the restoration of creation. Here Christ takes his disciples to the end of time and paints a picture of the climax of salvation. What is the salvation that will transform the world? Not a scrapping of the old, but "the renewal of all things." *Redemption* is another key word (*apolytrōsis*, used twenty-three times in the New Testament, with Romans 3:24 as a prime example of word usage). The meaning? To pay a ransom in order to buy a person back from captivity. The idea of restoring the old rather than escaping from or giving up on the old is at the heart of the concept of redemption. *Reconciliation (apokatallassō)* is a final example of a key word in the vocabulary of salvation that points to the restoring of creation and not the abandonment of it. It is used in Colossians 1:21-22 to describe the return of an alienated humanity to peace and harmonious relationship with God. In each of these key words the idea is central that salvation restores what was lost rather than abandons it.

2. The New Testament teaching about the kingdom of God supports the idea that salvation is the restoration of creation. Herman Ridderbos, in his *The Coming of the Kingdom,* calls the kingdom of God "the central theme of the whole revelation of God." The biblical usage does not refer primarily to a realm where God rules but to the fact of rulership. *Kingdom (basileia)* has as its primary meaning the right and power to rule and only secondarily the idea of a realm or region. Thus Christ defines the kingdom of God as his right to rule in Matthew 28:18: "All authority in heaven and on earth has been given to me." In the epistles the phrase *kingdom of God* (used frequently in the Gospels) thus is replaced by the

equivalent idea that Christ is Lord. Colossians 1 shows this clearly. In verse 13 Paul is praying for the Colossian believers, thanking God that "he has rescued us from the dominion of darkness and brought us into the kingdom of the Son he loves." What is this kingdom of the Son of God? Paul goes on in verses 15-19 to explain. *The kingdom* is another term for the lordship of Christ. Because Christ is Lord over all things as Creator and Sustainer, he is worthy of all praise and submission (vv. 15-16). But not only is he the Creator-King of verse 15, he is also the Redeemer-King of verses 18-19.

How does the redemptive rule and reign of Christ over all things support the idea of salvation as the restoration of creation rather than an abandoning of creation? Colossians makes this connection plain. Because Christ is the Creator of all things and "all things were made by him and for him," he refuses to allow the enemy to take permanently his good but fallen world. Instead of giving up on the work of his hands, Christ decides "to reconcile to himself all things, whether things on earth or things in heaven, by making peace through his blood, shed on the cross" (Col 1:20). This reconciling of all things means that Christ is going to restore the God-centered character of the cosmos as it was before the Fall. Christ's vast, supernatural resources are now being used to direct all of history toward this redemptive goal. This does not mean that every individual will be saved, but it does mean that a global, God-centered culture will one day dominate the earth.

This passage in Colossians 1 also teaches us about the scope of creation. In the light of Colossians 1:15-16, there is no area of human life that is outside Christ's lordship. Public education, world government, Hollywood, quantum physics, auto making, lovemaking, prayer, space exploration, the media—all are created and sustained by him and are capable of being renewed and transformed by him. We want to protect the lordship of Christ from any "two realm" thinking. Such thinking teaches that there are sacred things over which Christ is Lord and secular things over which he has little, if any, concern or control. We must oppose this type of dualism and speak instead of the comprehensive scope of his lordship.

What do we make of the areas of life that are full of rebellion and evil? How can Christ be Lord in these things? Do we not dishonor Christ by saying that he is Lord over abortion clinics and political injustice? These are good questions. The way to handle Christ's lordship over the rebellious areas and activities within his creation is to introduce the concept of antithesis. Antithesis simply means that all human actions can go in one of two ultimate directions. Human action can be either for God or for some other god, that is, for idols. Thinking antithetically means we never regard anything or anyone as "lower" or "higher" in value or regard some activities as inherently more "spiritual" than others. Antithesis teaches us that all things and actions can be spiritual (even fixing the plumbing) if they are directed toward the glory of God through Christ. Conversely, anything or anyone can be profane (even prayer and hymn singing) if it is directed away from the glory of the true and living God and toward idols. But even in light of the antithetical nature of the world around us (there is no morally neutral territory), Christ is still Lord. Christ will be Lord of judgment in instances of misdirection, "giving people up" to their idolatry and rebellion as Romans 1:18 teaches. At the same time, Christ is the redemptive Lord with sufficient power to raise the most repulsive reprobate and bring renewal, restoration, and reconciliation.

3. Finally, 2 Peter 3:10 supports the idea of salvation as the restoration of creation and not an escape from it. The reader may find this point puzzling, for perhaps no verse in the New Testament has been used more frequently than this to point to the destruction of creation and not the restoration of it. Listen to the fiery words of Peter: "But the day of the Lord will come like a thief. The heavens will disappear with a roar; the elements will be destroyed by fire, and the earth and everything in it will be laid bare." Other translations substitute "burned up" for "laid bare."

Doesn't this verse teach that creation will *not* be restored? Doesn't it seem to teach that creation will be annihilated? I think not for two reasons. First of all, the NIV translators accurately rendered the final verb of the verse. The verb is not *katakaiō* ("burned up") as the King James Version has it, but *heuriskō* ("discover" or "disclose"). This latter word is the basis for that quaint old word *eureka* associated in America with eccentric scientists or greedy gold miners. It carries the idea of having found or discovered something (often of value). The verse thus teaches that the fiery destruction in the heavens and on the earth at the time of Christ's return will be purgative, that is, cleansing all the remaining corruption from creation and removing the residual effects of the curse. Christ's Second Coming will thus "lay bare," or reveal, the true goodness of his creation marred for countless centuries by sin.

Second, the destruction on the day of the Lord (v. 10) is compared in verse 6 to the destruction of the world during the days of Noah. Now did the destruction of the earth in Noah's day mean that God abandoned his creation? No, it did not. The destruction of the earth in the flood was clearly not an abandoning of creation, but rather a cleansing of it. It is true that there was massive destruction of human life, of plant and animal life, and of landforms. But in every case God intended to restore the beauty and goodness of his creation through the purging by water. The future purging by fire (2 Pet 3:12) will accomplish the same thing and will issue in a new (that is, renewed) heaven and earth where righteousness dwells.

This is the vision of salvation reflected in our story. The uncle and the restored nephew will sprinkle the ashes of renewal and restoration over a Soweto desperately in need of new directions. But whose ashes are these, and what power do they possess? What do they teach about the centrality of the work of Christ in salvation? Our next point seeks to answer these questions.

Salvation Is Grounded in Christ

No more dramatic moment occurs in the story than when the uncle himself is transformed into an insect and then is killed by the mindless mob, who mistake him for the nephew. Christ became an insect for us. That he was God has already been discussed in our chapter on the Trinity. That he became one of us is the new fact that makes possible his death in our place (Jn 1:14; 3:16). He too was rejected and killed for us. This is the heart of the parable and is the ground of our salvation. We are not saved by learning new ideas. We are saved by someone's actions in history. These saving acts are the incarnation, crucifixion, resurrection, and ascension of Christ—the perfect mediator between God and humanity. I would like to look at the third (and arguable the most pivotal) of these four actions of Christ—the atonement for sins on the cross. What happened on Good Friday that restores me to God and cancels the wrath and condemnation against me that I so richly deserve? Five biblical words may help explain the power of the cross to save. Consider with me the cross of Christ as obedience, sacrifice, propitiation, reconciliation, and redemption.

Obedience. The obedience of Christ can be defined as his active and passive obedience to his Father's will on behalf of sinners. What do we mean? First of all, when we talk of Christ's passive obedience, we do not mean passive in the sense of involuntary—that Christ was forced by the Father to be our redeemer. Christ freely "offered himself up as a fragrant offering and sacrifice to God" (Eph 5:2). By "passive" we simply mean that Christ submitted to the penalties of the law for us. When Isaiah speaks in chapter 53 of his prophecy of the suffering servant who "was crushed for our iniquities," he is writing of the obedience of Christ. Although Christ was actively obeying the law of God while on the cross—in that he loved the Father with all his mind, soul, heart, and strength and loved his neighbor as himself—he was also obeying the law passively, meekly submitting to the penalties of the law deserved by me but graciously borne by himself (see also Jn 6:38, "I have come . . . to do the will of him who sent me"; and Jn 10:17-18; Heb 2:10-18; 5:8-10). The incarnation alone does not save. Mere death does not save. Death on the cross alone does not save. What saved a fallen humanity was death on the cross "as the climatic requirement of the price of redemption, . . . discharged as the supreme act of obedience; it was not death resistlessly inflicted but death upon the cross willingly and obediently wrought."[2] The saving power of the cross is forever tied to the fact that Christ's obedience was from the heart. To summarize, the message of the obedience of Christ is

> not something that may be conceived of artificially or abstractedly. It is obedience that enlisted all the resources of his perfect humanity, obedience that resided in his person, and obedience of which he is ever the perfect embodiment. . . . And we become the beneficiaries of it, indeed the partakers of it, by union with him. It is this that serves to advertise the significance of that which is the central truth of all soteriology, namely, union and communion with Christ.[3]

Sacrifice. What kind of sacrifice took place on the cross of Christ? Against the Old Testament background we can safely say that Christ offered himself up as a blood sacrifice as was offered on the day of atonement according to Leviticus 16, a sacrifice that was sufficient to cleanse Israel of whatever sins they had committed (Lev 16:16). These sacrifices (often the blood of a bull) were expiatory in that they dealt with sin and guilt and also substitutionary in that they were meant to take the place of the sinner. A third feature of the sacrifices offered on the day of atonement is that they were to be offered only by a duly appointed priest.

A major part of the argument of the book of Hebrews is that Christ's sacrifice meets the requirements of an acceptable sacrifice. Consider the teaching of Hebrews 9:14: "How much more, then, will the blood of Christ, who through the eternal Spirit offered himself unblemished to God, cleanse our consciences from acts that lead to death, so that we may serve the living God!"

Two of the three requirements of Leviticus 16 are met and exceeded by the sacrifice of Christ. First, Christ's sacrifice is supremely expiatory, cleansing the sinner perfectly of sin and guilt (in ways far superior to the animal sacrifices of the Old Testament). Second, Christ's sacrifice is substitutionary. He did not die for his own sins, for he was "unblemished," hence without sin. Thus the sacrifice of Christ meets or exceeds these two requirements of Leviticus 16. But what about the third requirement—the requirement of a duly appointed priest? Here the writer of Hebrews must deal with the embarrassing fact that Christ was not a Levite (he was from the tribe of Judah) and thus was apparently unqualified to offer himself up to God.

Hebrews 8 meets this objection head on. Christ is not a Levitical priest, admits the writer of Hebrews, but is still a priest, albeit of a higher order. Christ is a priest after the order of Melchizedek (cf. Ps 110:4, where God declares the future messiah to be a priest in this unique order). What this means for the author of the letter to the Hebrews is that Christ is an eternal priest (for Melchizedek, who appears briefly in Genesis to Abraham, is said never to die, unlike the mortal priests who make up the Levitical line of Aaron). This leads to the conclusion that

> such a high priest meets our need—one who is holy, blameless, pure, set apart from sinners, exalted above the heavens. Unlike the other high priests, he does not need to offer sacrifices day after day, first for his own sins, and then for the sins of the people. He sacrificed for their

sins once for all when he offered himself. For the law appoints as high priests men who are weak; but the oath [Ps 110:4], which came after the law, appointed the Son, who has been made perfect forever. (Heb 7:26-28)

Thus Christ meets the third requirement of being a duly appointed priest. His death on the cross is, therefore, the death of a perfect sacrifice offered up by an eternally appointed high priest. What is the outcome of this sacrifice? "He is able to save completely those who come to God through him" (Heb 7:25).

Propitiation. This word appears only in Romans 3:25 and 1 John 2:2 and 4:10. The basic meaning in each text is that Christ is the offering that satisfies the wrath of God against sin. If we talk of expiation as that which covers sins, then propitiation is that which satisfies God. *Propitiation* is a much more God-centered term for the saving power of the cross.

Some have objected that placating the wrath of God puts God in a bad light, for the God of the Bible is a loving God and not vengeful. Is that objection valid? Is the wrath of God inconsistent with the love of God? I can conclude on the basis of the Bible that holy love and holy vengeance are not incompatible. First John 4:10 comes to mind: "This is love: not that we loved God, but that he loved us and sent his Son as an atoning sacrifice [propitiation] for our sins." Propitiation is consistent with God's love, for it is the fruit of his love.

Propitiation adds greatly to our understanding of the saving power of the cross, for it demonstrates the radical God-centered nature of his love (cf. Rom 3:25) and the tremendous cost that redemptive love exacts within the family of the Trinity. John Murray explicates this:

God is love. But the supreme object of that love is himself. And because he loves himself supremely he cannot suffer what belongs to the integrity of his character and glory to be compromised or curtailed. That is the reason for the propitiation. God appeases his own holy wrath in the cross of Christ in order that the purpose of his love to lost men may be accomplished in accordance with and to the vindication of all the perfections that constitute his glory.[4]

Reconciliation. If propitiation deals with God's wrath over our sin, reconciliation deals with the overcoming of God's alienation from us due to our sin. Did I say God's alienation from us? Shouldn't I have said *our* alienation? In fact there are passages which show alienation to be in the mind of the person initiating the reconciliation, not in the enemy's heart or mind (Mt 5:23-24; Rom 11:15; 1 Cor 7:11). God thus changes the way he thinks about us because of the cross of Christ. This seems to be the burden of Romans 5:8-11, where Paul describes an objective reconciliation in the mind and heart of God before we experience subjectively the fruit of that reconciliation. The point here is that *reconciliation* is a good word to use for what Christ accomplished on the cross. If I just reserve it for what happens at my conversion, I will miss something far more foundational and wonderful, namely, "God demonstrates his own love for us in this: While we were still sinners, Christ died for us," and therefore "when we were God's enemies, we were reconciled to him through the death of his Son" (Rom 5:8, 10).

Redemption. The fifth and final word to describe the saving power of the cross is *redemption.* A general definition would go something like this: redemption is securing a release by payment of a price. In contrast to the other four words that we have looked at, the term *redemption* focuses on the bondage to sin that disobedience has created. But when Christ dies, the bondage is broken and the captors are now free. What bondage have we been freed from? We are free from the curse of the law (Gal 3:13), the penalty and power of sin (Heb 9:12), and the power of Satan.

If redemption is the securing of a release by payment, and we have been released from the curse of the law and the power of sin, then what was the payment? The answer shouts back to us from the whole New Testament: The redemptive payment was the death of the Mediator, Jesus Christ (Mk 10:45; Acts 20:28; Eph 1:7; Tit 2:14).

The ashes of the uncle in the story are an inadequate metaphor for the costly blood of Christ that saves us. How does it save us? It saves through the obedience that it represents, the sacrifice that it offers, the propitiation that it proffers, the reconciliation that it effects, and the redemption that it accomplishes. In light of these five great truths, I think of the words of the hymn "And Can It Be":

No condemnation now I dread;
Jesus, and all in him, is mine!
Alive in him, my living head,

And clothed in righteousness divine,
Bold I approach the eternal throne,
And claim the crown, through Christ my own.

Experiencing Christ and His Benefits

One of the most important moments in the parable occurs when the nephew experiences the impact of his uncle's death on his insect heart and life. Contact with both the death of the uncle and the risen life of the uncle restored the young man's true humanity and delivered him from his insectlike existence. In the same way faith in the power of the death and resurrection of Christ has a transforming impact on us, whose humanity has been horribly marred by the curse of sin. All the dimensions of alienation discussed in the previous chapter are reversed by these saving benefits of the death of Christ.

My own enjoyment of God flows from experiencing these transforming benefits of Christ. Many benefits could be mentioned, but I'd like to comment on just five that flow from the cross and the empty tomb: union with Christ, justification by faith, adoption, sanctification, and glorification.

Union with Christ. The first benefit of Christ's death for us, and the fountainhead of all others, is union with him by faith. As Bruce Milne explains: "The heart of Christian experience of the Holy Spirit lies in his bringing us into a living relationship to Jesus Christ so that we share in his redemption and all its benefits."[5] How important is union with Christ? Listen to the words of C. S. Lewis:

> Good things as well as bad, you know, are caught by a kind of infection. If you want to get warm you must stand by the fire; if you want to be wet you must get into the water. If you want joy, power, peace, eternal life, you must get close to, or even into, the thing that has them. . . . They are a great fountain of energy and beauty spurting up at the very center of reality. If you are close to it, the spray will wet you: if you are not, you will remain dry. Once a man is united to God, how could he not live forever?[6]

This union with Christ is neither physical nor sacramental. It is a spiritual union that is essentially relational. By the work of the Spirit uniting us to Christ and personally applying the death and resurrection of Christ to us, we "enjoy unfettered and unclouded fellowship with him, freed from every delusion of independence which would block the free flow of pure love, truth, trust, cooperative obedience and delight between [ourselves, our] creator and the other creatures."[7]

Galatians 2:20 describes this union graphically: "I have been crucified with Christ and I no longer live, but Christ lives in me. The life I live in the body, I live by faith in the Son of God, who loved me and gave himself for me." Commentator J. B. Lightfoot paraphrases Galatians 2:20 and the concept of personal identification with Christ's death and life: "When I speak of living, I do not mean myself, my natural being. I have no longer a separate existence. I am merged with Christ."[8]

What does this "merger" with Christ actually mean? Because we belong to Christ by faith, all that he accomplished in his death and resurrection is shared with us. Our life in Christ is to live by faith in him at every moment. Luther, writing in 1520, described this faith-union with Christ in terms of a marriage:

> Faith unites the soul with Christ as a bride is united with her bridegroom. As Paul teaches us, Christ and the soul become one flesh by this mystery (Ephesians 5:31-32). And if they are one flesh and the marriage is real . . . then it follows that everything that they have is held in common, whether good or evil. So the believer can boast of and glory of whatever Christ possesses as though it were his or her own; and whatever the believer has, Christ claims as his own. . . . Christ is full of grace, life and salvation. The human soul is full of sin, death and damnation. Now let faith come between them. Sin, death and damnation will be Christ's. And grace, life and salvation will be the believer's.[9]

This exchanged life made possible by a marital-like union with Christ prompted Luther to call faith "a wedding ring"—that which formally seals the union of bride and groom.

Every other saving benefit comes to us by this union with Christ through the Spirit. Because of this union every imaginable benefit shall be ours. The golden chain of Romans 8:30-32 promises: "And those he predestined, he also called; those he called, he also justified; those he justified, he also glorified. What, then, shall we say in response to this? If God is for us, who can be against us? He who did not spare his own

Son, but gave him up for us all—how will he not also, along with him, graciously give us all things?" Verse 32 contains what must surely be one of the greatest rhetorical questions in the Bible: "How will he not also, along with him, graciously give us all things"? The answer of course is that there is no possible way those for whom Christ died and who have been placed by the work of the Holy Spirit into an indestructible faith-union with Christ can fail to enjoy justification, sanctification and glorification (and all other benefits of Christ). All things that Christ has purchased for his bride will be given to and enjoyed fully by the bride.

Justification by faith. Union with Christ is the foundation of a second powerful benefit—the grand experience of full acceptance by God known as justification by faith. The salvation of the young insect depended upon the total and costly love of the uncle for him, even when the nephew was repulsive in his ugliness. But the next step was that the nephew was declared fully human ("right") even when he was still an insect.

The basic concept of justification is clear enough—to reward and vindicate someone from charges of wrongdoing on the basis of his or her good life and reputation. As James Buchanan writes: "By Justification we mean—man's acceptance with God, or his being regarded and treated as righteous in His sight—as the object of favour and not of His wrath; of His blessing and not of His curse."[10]

This definition sounds good until we begin to talk of the justification of sinners. If to justify means (as it properly should mean) to reward or vindicate those who do what is right, then how can we speak of rewarding the undeserving and unjust? This is logically and morally contradictory. We might as well speak of square circles or the construction of a judicial system designed to reward criminals for being kind enough to inflict their misery and suffering upon society.

The scandal of the justification of sinners makes sense only in light of union with Christ. By this "royal marriage" (Luther), we exchange our sins with Christ and receive his righteousness as though it were our own. The Father's opinion of us now is that we are free from sin and right in his sight by virtue of the death of Christ covering sins and imputing (crediting) his righteousness to us.

This leads us now to a definition of Christian justification. Justification by faith in Christ can be defined as "the declared purpose of God to regard and treat those sinners who believe in the Lord Jesus Christ as if they had not sinned, on the ground of the merits of Christ."[11]

This understanding of justification by faith in Christ is supported by Galatians 2:15-16 (among other texts): "We who are Jews by birth and not 'Gentile sinners' know that a man is not justified by observing the law, but by faith in Jesus Christ. So we, too, have put our faith in Christ Jesus that we may be justified by faith in Christ and not by observing the law, because by observing the law no one will be justified."[12]

Note four things about the justification spoken of here in Galatians. First, note what justification is *not*. It is not my acceptance by God on the basis of good deeds, conscientious law-keeping, focusing on the family, regular churchgoing or sacrificial social action. I cannot boast of anything that I have done to win this favorable verdict from God. Second, note what it *is*. Justification is being in right relation with God through faith in Christ. God gives to us through the death of Christ that which we could not earn ourselves—eternal life and union with him. Faith is the empty hand that receives this freely offered gift. Third, justification looks to the past when it pardons all my previous sins. They are blotted out and remembered by God no more. Fourth, justification is more than past pardon; it is anchored in the future. "Justification has respect to the law, and to God's *future dealings* with the sinner. It is an act by which God determines to treat him hereafter as a righteous man, or *as if* he had not sinned. The ground or reason of this is the merit of the Lord Jesus Christ—merit such that we can plead it *as if* it were our own."[13] Thus in justification the last judgment of God at the end of time has broken into the midst of time, into my time, and foretold to me what that final verdict will be—"not guilty but righteous forever in God's eyes by virtue of faith in Christ."[14]

Adoption. Adoption can be defined as "that work of God's grace by which he receives us as his very own children through Christ and in union with him."[15] As great as the previous benefits of the cross have been, there remains a special wonder to the grace of adoption, for

> when we recall what we were in our sins, the thought of adoption speaks most powerfully of the magnitude of God's mercy to us. That we should be pardoned all our sins is wonder enough; but that

pardoned rebels should become God's very sons and daughters, installed within the intimacy of his own family circle, is surely wonder beyond wonder.[16]

A central text on adoption is Galatians 4:4-7:

> But when the time had fully come, God sent his Son, born of a woman, born under law, to redeem those under law, that we might receive the full rights of sons. Because you are sons, God sent the Spirit of his Son into our hearts, the Spirit who calls out, "*Abba,* Father." So you are no longer a slave, but a son; and since you are a son, God has made you also an heir.

Note a number of truths about adoption presented in this passage. First, adoption is purchased by the death of Christ. Second, adoption goes beyond forgiveness to a full and final acceptance by the Triune God as a member of the family. By adoption we have all the rights and privileges that Christ (in his humanity) has as a son of God ("full rights of sons").

Third, adoption means that the Spirit fills my life with an indestructible and soul-satisfying sense of the never-ending love of the Father for me ("*Abba,* Father"). At the heart of this tender cry is the truth that my aversion to God, the rage against the music that the noise of the crows produces, is being lifted. Where there was God-suppression and suspicion there is now a growing whisper of intimacy, warmth, confidence and joyous love. I am given this unshakable assurance that nothing can separate me from the love of God (Rom 8:38-39). This full assurance, when it is experienced, is the maximum experience of joy in life: "you will fill me with joy *in your presence,* with eternal pleasures *at your right hand.*" Adoption gives intimacy with the One who is joy itself.

Fourth, adoption gives us the privilege of confident prayer. The Spirit produces a wonderful life of prayer in the heart of God's adopted children. We, through the Spirit, pray to "Abba, Father." Such prayer was unknown in Jewish devotional literature before the coming of Christ. Jesus further taught us to pray to "our Father, who is in Heaven." Because we are children of God we can "approach the throne of grace with confidence, so that we may receive mercy and find grace to help us in our time of need" (Heb 4:16).

Finally, adoption means I am an heir. All things will be ours as sons and daughters of God through union with Christ. Every need of life and eternity will be met, every hunger of body and soul will be satisfied, for when it comes to those who are his sons, "my God will meet all your needs according to his glorious riches in Christ Jesus" (Phil 4:19).

Sanctification. A fourth benefit flowing from the death of Christ is sanctification. This grace can be defined as that work of the Holy Spirit in those who are in faith-union with Christ "whereby the heart becomes holy and is made after God's own heart."[17] This benefit is portrayed in our parable when the nephew undergoes his restoration to full humanity.

Let me begin to explain this transforming benefit by making two important distinctions. The first distinction is between *definitive* and *progressive* sanctification. There is an important sense in which sanctification is "definitive"—that is, a one-time gift of God at conversion when we are made his very own possession. We become "holy" or "sanctified" in the sense of being in the Holy One—Jesus Christ—and by belonging to the Holy God. But the other side of this distinction is that progressive sanctification is still a reality, flowing out from this definitive or positional sanctification. This latter aspect of sanctification refers to the daily and ongoing warfare of the believer throughout his or her life against indwelling sin and the fallen world system without.

The second distinction is between *mortification* and *vivification.* Mortification is the negative part of sanctification which "deadens" sinful attitudes and actions in our lives (what the Puritans called "mortifying" sin) in order to remove the stain and corruption of sin from us. Vivification is the positive part of sanctification which involves cultivating holy, Christlike attitudes and actions in all of our life.

One of the great chapters on sanctification is Romans 6. We can see the distinctions noted above (between definitive and progressive sanctification and positive and negative aspects of sanctification) woven together in Paul's discussion. The chapter contains Paul's answer to an imagined objection to justification by faith in Christ alone: "Shall we go on sinning so that grace may increase?" (Rom 6:1). Paul's answer is a resounding no, because the believer is "dead to sin but alive to God" (Rom 6:11). In what sense are we dead to sin and alive to God? Paul gives four senses in which sanctification (dying to sin and rising to holy, God-centered living) is true for every believer.[18]

First, we died to sin in a *judicial sense.* This means that we are holy and without sin in God's sight because he sees us in union with Christ, who died to remove our sins and rose to give us new life. Romans 6:6-8 speaks of this first sense of sanctification: "For we know that our old self was crucified with him so that the body of sin might be done away with, that we should no longer be slaves to sin—because anyone who has died has been freed from sin. Now if we died with Christ, we believe that we will also live with him." God's decision to nail our sins to the cross of Christ means that he has decided to look at us now as sinless (our sins having been *judicially* removed). Sanctification in this judicial sense is virtually identical to justification.

Second, we died to sin in a *baptismal sense.* "Don't you know that all of us who were baptized into Christ Jesus were baptized into his death?" (Rom 6:3). The idea here is not that baptism makes us holy but that it is the formal ratification of the pledge of Christ and his death to the believer. By public baptism I am officially accepting my death to sin in Christ's death and committing myself to live new life because I am alive in Christ. Baptism is my promise to turn from sin and live for Christ. At the same time baptism is a testimony that the saving grace of God is in my life to empower me to keep my promise.

Third, we died to sin in a *moral sense.* This refers to progressive sanctification—the moment-by-moment moral decision-making that the believer engages in when confronted by the ethical dilemmas and temptations of life. Romans 6:12-14 defines this third sense of sanctification:

> Therefore do not let sin reign in your mortal body so that you obey its evil desires. Do not offer the parts of your body to sin, as instruments of wickedness, but rather offer yourselves to God, as those who have been brought from death to life; and offer the parts of your body to him as instruments of righteousness. For sin shall not be your master, because you are not under law, but under grace.

The believer, as C. E. B. Cranfield explains, has "been given the freedom to die daily and hourly to sin by the mortification of their sinful natures, and to rise daily and hourly to newness of life in obedience to God."[19] What Paul leaves out of Romans 6 but includes in Romans 8 is the central role of the Holy Spirit in this moral decision-making: "For if you live according to the sinful nature, you will die; but if by the Spirit you put to death the misdeeds of the body, you will live" (Rom 8:13).

Fourth, we died to sin in a *future sense.* In Romans 6:5 Paul speaks of the fact that "we will certainly also be united with him in his resurrection." The day is coming in which sanctification will be completed and in which we, who have died to sin in Christ, will die to sin and rise to new life in a final and full way. "They will die to sin finally and irreversibly when they actually die, and will—equally finally and irreversibly—at Christ's coming be raised up to the resurrection life."[20]

With the mention of sanctification in the future we are at the door of the fifth great benefit of the death of Christ—glorification. But first some words of warning are needed. We must not neglect Christian hedonism in our fight against sin. Instead, we must learn how to fight desire with desire. We must learn how to fight pleasure with pleasure. Holiness is the renunciation of lesser pleasures in order to gain greater (eternal) ones. Sin is the renunciation of eternal pleasures for lesser ones. When God becomes my supreme treasure, no preacher needs to tell me to give up lesser things that would stand between my longing and my treasure, for "where your treasure is, there your heart will be also" (Mt 6:21). When God is finally discovered as life's greatest pleasure, the believer will no longer need the lash of rebuke to leave unworthy pleasures. Fighting the pleasures of sin with the pleasures of God is the moral logic of the apostle Paul in Philippians 3:8: "What is more, I consider everything a loss compared to the surpassing greatness of knowing Christ Jesus my Lord, for whose sake I have lost all things. I consider them rubbish, that I may gain Christ." Paul overcame sin by wanting something that surpassed sin in its beauty and allure—namely, knowing Christ. Thus Christian hedonism is crucial in the process of sanctification. This is the secret of godliness.

A second warning concerns the temptation to go to extremes in our reaction to the world of creation and culture. When we speak of dying to sin and cultivating holiness, we must avoid thinking on the one hand in terms of a *world-denying spirituality* that attacks the goodness of God's world of creation and culture or on the other hand of an *uncritical world-affirming spirituality.* Some monks and ascetics are examples of the former. Health-and-wealth Christianity is an example of the latter. Biblical sanctification calls us to a third way that might be called *critical world-affirming spirituality.*[21] Paul's words in Philippians 3 could be construed to mean that the world of creation and culture is a world of junk that we should be glad to throw away. Paul means quite the opposite of that. Christ was such a surpassing treasure that nothing was as valuable as knowing Christ. All other treasures are meager and shabby (though still retaining value) in comparison with the splendor of the riches to be found in Christ. Paul's statement in Philippians 3:8 must be put alongside his statement in 1 Timothy 4:4 that "everything God created is good, and nothing is to be rejected if it is received with thanksgiving."

A critical world-affirming spirituality thus avoids an inordinate love of this world by focusing on the greater wealth found in eternal things while at the same time growing in appreciation for the good things God has given. The Quaker leader William Penn echoed this conviction when he said that "true godliness does not turn men out of the world, but enables them to live better in it, and excites their endeavors to mend it."[22] We must use the world of creation and culture as pilgrims on a journey, not becoming so entangled in the love of the things around us that we forget that we are on a journey to the Celestial City. But like pilgrims seeking to maximize their joy in the God of the journey, we are to take the things of the world and "possess, enjoy and use them, with no other view but readily to quit them, whenever we are called to it, and to change them willingly for heaven."[23]

Glorification. Our parable ended with the nephew assisting his uncle in working for the "coming metamorphosis." The ultimate transformation of this good but fallen world will occur only at the end of history. Thus, the great chain of saving benefits listed in Romans 8:30 ends with the gift of glorification. Glorification may be defined as that act of God the Holy Spirit at the end of history whereby he completes the work of perfecting all things in Christ (Eph 1:10). This transformation attends the second coming of Christ to earth to assume his visible rule and reign. Morally, mentally, physically and relationally "we shall be like him, for we shall see him as he is" (1 Jn 3:2). In cosmic terms, glorification has a message of hope for all of creation and culture (Rom 8:21-22). Consider five aspects of glorification and how each speaks of the culmination of Christian hedonism in the perfecting of our enjoyment of God.

First, glorification means transformed bodies. Philippians 3:20-21 reminds us that "our citizenship is in heaven. And we eagerly await a Savior from there, the Lord Jesus Christ, who, by the power that enables him to bring everything under his control, will transform our lowly bodies so that they will be like his glorious body." Someday these bodies, so prone to age and decay, will be gloriously transformed into new immortal bodies that will never grow weary or die. Thus a greater capacity to enjoy God, to pursue the pleasure of his company and service without heaviness, sickness or fatigue, will be ours.

Second, glorification means transformed hearts. The promise of 1 John 3:2 ("we know that when he appears, we shall be like him") is spoken in the context of overcoming sin (v. 3). The impact of removing sin from our hearts will be breathtaking—freeing us to love one another completely.

Third, glorification means a transformed mind. "Now I know in part; then I shall know fully, even as I am fully known" (1 Cor 13:12). This passage promises that all the mental obstacles to the enjoyment of God and his love—all the unbelief and dualistic thinking, all the fussy opinions and nasty dichotomies between knowing and doing—will be overcome and my mind transformed. The words of praise that I grope for, often in vain; the mental images of God's beauty and glory that I strain without success to paint in language; the thimble-sized clichés that I fall back on to capture the skyline of his excellencies—all these will be replaced by a mental vitality that I can now only imagine with holy envy. "There shall be no want . . . of words wherewith to praise the object of their affection. Nothing shall hinder them from communing with God, and praising and serving him just as their love inclines them to do."[24]

Fourth, glorification means transformed relationships. First Corinthians 13:13 speaks of the reign of love in eternity: "And now these three remain: faith, hope and love. But the greatest of these is love." This reign and triumph of love will transform our relationships with God and others. There will be a perfecting of our love to God. "In heaven there shall be no remaining enmity, or distaste, or coldness, or deadness of heart towards God. . . . As the saints will love God with an inconceivable ardency of heart, and to the utmost of their capacity, so they will know that he has loved them from all eternity, and still loves them, and will continue to love them for ever."[25] There will also be a similar perfecting of our relationships with others. Edwards describes the beauty of this "world of love" where the love of each for the other is without blemish or sham:

Heavenly lovers will have no doubt of the love of each other. They shall have no fear that the declarations and professions of love are hypocritical; but shall be perfectly satisfied of the sincerity and strength of each other's affection, as much as if there were a window in every breast, so that everything in the heart could be seen. . . . Everyone will be just what he seems to be, and will really have all the love that he seems to have.[26]

Fifth, glorification means a transformed world. Revelation 21:1-2 describes the transformed cosmos after the return of Christ. "Then I saw a new heaven and a new earth, for the first heaven and the first earth had passed away, and there was no longer any sea. I saw the Holy City, the new Jerusalem, coming down out of heaven from God, prepared as a bride beautifully dressed for her husband." We do not know what this new heaven and new earth and holy city will really be like. But we know that the beauty awaiting us there will be beyond that which we have found in this life; that the joys of that redeemed creation and culture will exceed the joys of this present time; and that the meaning of time will be altered from the world-weary clock and calendar watching that dulls us now to a never-ending morning that is always filled with the freshness of dawn.

"Everyone who has this hope in him purifies himself, just as he is pure" (1 Jn 3:3).

Enjoying the Truths of Redemption

We leave our friends in the parable, having gathered plates of food mingled with ashes, to work for the coming metamorphosis. Which leads to another question: what does a transformed world look like? We could describe it in terms of what will be missing—no sin, no tears, no crime, no poverty. We could also describe it in terms of what it will include. For my money the leading indicator of a world transformed is a world ablaze with praise. The apostle John was given a peek of just such a metamorphosis in Revelation, and the vision was white-hot with worship: "Each of the four living creatures had six wings and was covered with eyes all around, even under his wings. Day and night they never stop saying: "Holy, holy, holy is the Lord God Almighty, who was, and is, and is to come" (Rev 4:8). But however intense was the worship of God as Creator, it is superseded in the next scene in heaven by the joy that flows from seeing God as Redeemer:

> Then I looked and heard the voice of many angels, numbering thousands upon thousands, and ten thousand times ten thousand. They encircled the throne and the living creatures and the elders. In a loud voice they sang: "Worthy is the Lamb, who was slain, to receive power and wealth and wisdom and strength and honor and glory and praise!" Then I heard every creature in heaven and on earth and under the earth and on the sea, and all that is in them, singing: "To him who sits on the throne and to the Lamb be praise and honor and glory and power, for ever and ever!" (Rev 5:11-13)

If theology is the art and science of enjoying God through Christ in all of life, then the truths of salvation are the best fuel for our enjoyment of our Triune God. Three points come to my mind when I ask myself how the truths of redemption can fuel my passion for God.

Knowing God as Redeemer in Christ fills me with the joy and relief that comes from personal deliverance. When Luther found relief for his battered conscience in the truths of justification by faith in Christ, he wrote that it was as though the "gates of paradise had opened." Never had he known such joy in God, who finally had a "friendly face" in Christ. For Luther, the cross was a tragedy that produced ecstasy. David would have understood Luther. In Psalm 30 we find the poet-politician preparing for the worship and enjoyment of his God by considering the personal redemption that he has been given:

> I will exalt you, O LORD, for you lifted me out of the depths and did not let my enemies gloat over me. O LORD my God, I called to you for help and you healed me. O LORD, you brought me up from the grave; you spared me from going down into the pit. Sing to the LORD, you saints of his; praise his holy name. For his anger lasts only a moment, but his favor lasts a lifetime; weeping may remain for a night, but rejoicing comes in the morning. (Ps 30:1-5)

When we acknowledge the depth of our sin, as the parable of Ratty, Mole, and the magic flute sought to help us do, we are prepared to experience the joy of deliverance in Christ. My own enjoyment of God is almost daily enriched by the redemptive truths of Galatians 2:20 and the confidence that my Heavenly Father brings me low only to lift me high and give me the satisfaction in God that comes from fresh glimpses of his work as Redeemer. As I face death, sickness, and suffering with him and not without him, my comfort and gladness that he is for me and not against me reach a crescendo.

The joy of worship increases when I know the redemptive heart of God. How can I make my public worship more meaningful and vital? Many churches are working through that question. One common answer is to put more emphasis on the transcendence and majesty of God in our songs and worship themes. We certainly need more of this, but my fear (voiced earlier in the chapter on Harlowe and the majesty of God) is that we will develop a piety of glory that produces spiritual pride ("look at my lofty thoughts of God") and little real enjoyment of God himself. Others may be filled with more carnal fear than worship, for as they focus on a God who is all-powerful and eternal, they may wonder whether this awesome being is for us or against us. The attributes of God can produce as much terror as joy if we try to stare at them directly without going through the cross.

But what happens when we focus more on our sin and Christ's powerful remedy in the cross to the problem of sin? When I approach God and his attributes from that perspective, some wonderful things that happened to Isaiah in chapter 6 of his prophecy happen to me. Although he saw the glory of God in the midst of the cherubim, his reaction is one of personal depression and despair—not joy. Only when the holy one approached him with the fiery coal of redemption and cleansing from sin and spoke the transforming words "your guilt is taken away and your sin atoned for" did Isaiah respond with worship and glad submission (Is 6:1-8). The joy of worship increases when I know the redemptive heart of God.

Like Isaiah, I should respond to seeing the heart of God by embracing his mission. "Here am I. Send me" was the response of an overjoyed sinner. Why does Romans 12:1 keeping ringing in my ears? "Therefore, I urge you brothers, in view of God's mercy, to offer your bodies as living sacrifices, holy and pleasing to God—this is your spiritual act of worship."

My joy in God increases as I consider the hope of heaven and the final consummation. Jonathan Edwards once described heaven as "a world of love" and increased his own joy in God not just by noting present blessings but also by anticipating the future pleasures of that "world of love." He meditated on the joy of having sin completely purged from our lives and the new capacity to enjoy God, one another, and the creation around us that purging would make possible. Such a thought does increase my joy.

But even beyond heaven, I look forward to the day of his coming, when "the earth will be filled with the knowledge of the glory of the LORD, as the waters cover the sea" (Hab 2:14). That is the whole point of enjoying God. My chief end is to glorify God by enjoying him. To see him given the worth and praise due to his name at last will be my highest joy and pleasure. Such a meditation helps me to face life's little disappointments with a "so what" attitude. So what if the tire goes flat, or the promotion at work falls through, or the American dream doesn't come true for me? Above and beyond the tired and temporal fantasies of my semisanctified imagination stands a greater vision of the final triumph of the kingdom of God on the earth over all its enemies. The dreams that will be fulfilled on that day are enough to savor forever.

Conclusion

When Luther lay down to die in the year 1546, he began to mutter over and over words that could barely be heard. Those who attended him bent low to hear. What would be the last words of this giant of a theologian whose writings would fill more than a hundred volumes in the German edition and whose ideas had changed the world? What final profundity would he utter? As his friends and family strained to hear Luther's dying thoughts, each soon recognized the words that came from his pale lips: "For God so loved the world he gave his only son, that whosoever believes in him should not perish but have everlasting life." Over and over again, until silence enfolded him, Luther repeated the words of John 3:16. There is no deeper truth. There is no greater key to unlock the enjoyment of God. There is no plan of history any greater than that contained in this verse. Redemption is the last and greatest act of the drama that begins with creation, staggers through the Fall, and culminates on the cross.

The parable of the insect sought to present this truth. In the commentary I reviewed four points hinted at in the parable: that salvation is the restoration of creation (and not an escape from creation), that salvation is grounded in the redemptive work of Christ in history, that the death of Christ gives us saving benefits, and that awareness of our redemption is the key to enjoying God through Christ in all of life.

With the discussion of these points about redemption, our task is finished. The opening chapter called us to find a way to increase our joy in God. Theological truth is a great ally in that quest, and consequently we have been doing theology for the last eight chapters. I defined theology as the art and science of enjoying God through Christ in all of life. Because I wanted our theology to challenge our worldview convictions, I employed a different approach to doing theology, something called narrative theology. The hope was that biblical truth presented in both stories and commentary would make a greater impact on our basic beliefs about things.

We have been guided by five convictions about God and his world that we have explored in story and in Scripture. I repeat them for the final time. If I am to glorify God by enjoying him, then I must confess:

The ultimate authority of the Bible. How can I know the truth? I am headed in the right direction when I affirm in heart and in mind that the triune God has spoken, generally through creation and history, but in a special way through Christ in the Scriptures. The Scriptures, therefore, are the written Word of God and are the error-free source of ultimate truth in all areas of life and reality.

The majesty and Trinity of God. What is the heart of reality? I am headed in the right direction when I affirm in heart and mind that the triune God is the heart of reality. From the mutual self-giving and joy that each member of the Trinity finds in the other comes the God-centered love that is behind the creation of all things, the judgment on all things, and the redemption of all things that God has chosen to redeem.

The goodness and comprehensiveness of creation. Why am I here? I am headed in the right direction when I affirm in heart and mind that the triune God has created all things, including history and culture as well as the natural world, and that they are good because God has made them. Humanity was created in God's image as male and female in order to love him and build God-centered cultures. Central to this task is the institution of marriage and the family.

The cosmic scope of the Fall and sin. What's wrong with me and my world? I am headed in the right direction when I affirm in heart and mind that the human creature has rebelled against the triune God's purpose for human life (God-centered culture building) and that this rebellion is cosmic in scope, extending to humanity's being, society and culture, history and religion. The primary expression of this rebellion is idolatry. Because of this rebellion and idolatry, suffering, evil, and death have been unleashed into human experience. The goodness of creation and culture has been horribly misdirected, being used now for idols rather than for God.

The fullness of redemption in Christ. What's the solution to life's problems and the curse that hangs over life? I am headed in the right direction when I affirm in heart and mind that the triune God has not given up on creation, history, and culture, but has chosen to restore and perfect his good but fallen world, transforming it into the kingdom of God where righteousness and peace will dwell. The kingdom of God (the restoration of all things through the lordship of Christ) is established through the Redeemer, Jesus Christ, who, through his death and resurrection and the renewing work of the Holy Spirit, creates a new people of God, the church, as witnesses to the kingdom.

These are the truths that will move us toward glorifying God by enjoying him.

I would like to tell one last parable. It seems that there was once a certain wise man who built his house on solid rock. When the rains came and the creek rose and the winds blew, this man was safe and snug and full of joy in his house on the rock. It did not fall, because it had its foundation on solid rock. But there was this other man who thought he knew a shortcut. Rather than do the hard work of carving out a strong and square foundation in an unyielding layer of granite, this man thought he would build his house on the sand. It was simple to do. The house went up in record time. When the rains came and the creek rose and the winds blew, something terrible happened. The house that was built in the sand crashed.

I'm tempted to offer a comment on this final parable. That is what I've done with all the other parables in this book. But I won't. I think you get the point.

Questions for Individuals or for Group Discussion

Part One

1. What caused the young man in this story to become an insect?

Is sin really hatred? Explain.

Can someone actually hate God? Explain.

Is there any biblical basis for these ideas? (Look at Romans 1:18-28.)

The parable pictures God as judging the hatred by giving people up to it. Is that an accurate picture of the wrath of God, letting people do what they want and experience the consequences? Explain.

2. What do we learn about the uncle in this story? In what ways does he reflect the Mediator, Jesus Christ?

In what ways is he dissimilar?

3. How does the uncle try to help his nephew early in the story?

What does he reveal about the meaning of sin and salvation in his argument with the mob?

4. How does this parable depict the death of the uncle? Compare and contrast the uncle's death with the death of Christ.

Christ's death on the cross has been understood as an example for us, as a payment for our sin and as a dramatic fight with the powers of evil. How is the death of Christ understood in this parable?

How does Romans 3:23-26 explain the death of Christ?

Are the ideas found in Romans 3 reflected in the parable, or are they missing from the parable?

5. How was the nephew restored to true humanity?

What is the significance of his rolling in the ashes and of the ashes' choking off his angry protests against God and others?

How do we unleash the power of Christ's death in our own lives?

6. Why did the neighbors become insects?

What is the "coming metamorphosis" mentioned at the end of the story?

What would bring about their restoration?

How does bringing the benefits of Christ to others restore our own true humanity?

7. What does this parable teach you about the cross?

What does it teach about our response to the cross?

What does it teach about living daily with an awareness and appreciation of the death of Christ?

How would such an awareness help us become fully human?

Part Two

8. Why is it important to affirm that salvation is the restoration of creation and not an escape from creation?

What are some ways that dualism can creep into our view of salvation?

What are the most useful arguments for supporting the comprehensive scope of redemption?

9. Review the five words that describe the saving power of the cross. Which words get to the heart of our salvation for you?

Which words are easier to communicate to others in our culture?

10. Which of the five benefits of knowing Christ fill you with the most gratitude? Which benefits do you need to understand and enjoy more deeply?

What new ideas presented here could deepen your delight in knowing Christ?

11. Which of the three ways of fueling delight in God as Redeemer appeals the most to you?

How would deepening your faith in conviction number five increase your satisfaction in God?

12. What does the final parable mean for you?

What actions do you need to take to strengthen your theological foundations for an eternity of enjoying God?

For Further Reading

To pursue the teaching on redemption introduced in this chapter I recommend the following books: John Murray, *Redemption Accomplished and Applied* (Grand Rapids: Eerdmans, 1955); Sinclair Ferguson, *The Christian Life* (London: Hodder and Stoughton, 1981); John Stott, *The Cross of Christ* (Downers Grove, Ill.: IVP, 1986); and Alister McGrath, *Justification: Its Meaning for Today* (Grand Rapids: Zondervan, 1989). Together these books cover the objective basis of our redemption in Christ as well as our subjective experience of it through the work of the Holy Spirit.

Notes

Chapter One/Doing Theology: The Trouble with Ralph

[1] John Calvin, *Institutes of the Christian Religion,* ed. John T. McNeill, 2 vols. (Philadelphia: Westminster, 1960), 35, 37.

[2] Millard Erickson, *Christian Theology* (Grand Rapids: Baker, 1987), 28.

[3] Paul Vitz, *Psychology as Religion: The Cult of Self-Worship* (Grand Rapids: Eerdmans, 1977), 100.

[4] Erickson, *Christian,* 1244.

[5] G. K. Chesterton, *Orthodoxy* (New York: Doubleday, 1908).

[6] Thomas Watson, *A Body of Divinity* (Grand Rapids: Sovereign Grace, n.d.; orig. 1692), 3.

[7] *Idem.*

[8] Ian Breward, ed., *The Work of William Perkins* (Appleford, England: Sutton Courtenay Press, 1970), 177.

[9] John Piper, *Desiring God: Meditations of a Christian Hedonist* (Portland: Multnomah Press, 1986).

[10] Ibid., 18.

[11] Watson, *Body,* 5.

[12] D. Wright, "Theology," in *New Dictionary of Theology,* ed. Sinclair Ferguson and David Wright (Downers Grove, Ill.: InterVarsity Press, 1988), 681.

[13] Martin Luther, "Heidelberg Disputation," in *Luther: Early Theological Works,* ed. James Atkinson (Philadelphia: Westminster, 1962), 290-91.

[14] Albert Wolters, *Creation Regained: Biblical Basics for a Reformational Worldview* (Grand Rapids: Eerdmans, 1985), 7-8.

Chapter Two/Scripture: The Gift of Arthur

[1] John J. Davis, *Foundations of Evangelical Theology* (Grand Rapids: Baker, 1984), 75.

[2]Bruce Milne, *Know the Truth* (Downers Grove, Ill.: InterVarsity Press, 1982), 20.

[3]Ibid., 35.

[4]See Erickson, *Christian,* 206-7, for a fuller discussion of these views.

[5]Milne, *Know,* 35.

[6]Donald Bloesch, *Essentials of Evangelical Theology* (New York: Harper & Row, 1978) 1:75.

[7]Jack Davis adds this note to Psalm 18:30: "The word translated here as 'flawless' is a participial form of the verb . . . used in reference to purging gold or silver by fire, and to separate from dross. . . . The implication is that God's word is free from all dross and impurities." Davis, *Handbook of Basic Bible Texts* (Grand Rapids: Baker, 1984), 18.

[8]See Erickson, *Christian,* 222.

[9]Piper, *Desiring,* 118.

[10]Ibid., 118.

[11]Milne, *Know,* 50.

Chapter Three/The Trinity: The Pride of Simba

[1]*Philadelphia Confession of Faith* (1720) 2. 3.

[2]Milne, *Know,* 59.

[3]See the discussion in Erickson, *Christian,* 328.

[4]For a full discussion of Arius's views see J. N. D. Kelly, *Early Christian Doctrines* (New York: Harper & Row, 1959), 226ff.

[5]Quoted in ibid., 232.

[6]John Piper, *The Pleasures of God* (Portland: Multnomah Press, 1991), 38.

[7]Cornelius Plantinga, "The Divine Family," *Christianity Today,* March 4, 1988, p. 27.

[8]Donald Kauffman, ed., *Favorite Christian Poems* (Old Tappan, N.J.: Revell, 1969), 17.

[9]C. S. Lewis, *A Mind Awake,* ed. Clyde S. Kilby (New York: Harcourt Brace Jovanovich, 1968), 210.

[10]Ibid., 106.

[11]Ibid.

Chapter Four/The Attributes of God: Harlowe's Biggest Case

[1]"The *dynamic* ontology of the Bible clashes inevitably with the *static* ontology of the Greek thinkers, so that when the two visions of reality are brought together, biblical teaching becomes warped and twisted and the resultant synthesis doctrinally objectionable." Clark Pinnock, "The Need for a Scriptural, and Therefore a Neo-Classical Theism," in *Perspectives on Evangelical Theology,* ed. Kenneth Kantzer and Stanley Gundry (Grand Rapids: Baker, 1979), 41.

[2]See *The Book of Confessions* (New York: General Assembly of the United Presbyterian Church USA, 1967).

[3]James Garrett, *Systematic Theology* (Grand Rapids: Eerdmans, 1990), 1:224.

[4]Paul Althaus, *Theology of Martin Luther* (Philadelphia: Fortress, 1968), 34.

[5]Ibid.

[6]See *Book of Confessions.*

[7]Milne, *Know,* 65.

[8]John Piper in his exegetical study of Romans 9:1-23 defines the righteousness of God as "his unswerving commitment always to preserve the honor of his name and display his glory." Piper, *The Justification of God* (Grand Rapids: Baker, 1983), 203.

[9]Quoted in ibid., 69.

[10]Erickson, *Christian,* 283ff.

[11]Piper, *Desiring,* 65.

[12]Ibid., 78.

Chapter Five/Creation: The Last Adventure of Ebenezer Scrooge

[1]Bruce Milne has a brief but useful discussion of the various views of Genesis 1 and the days of creation in *Know the Truth.*

[2]Quoted in Langdon Gilkey, *Maker of Heaven and Earth* (Garden City, N.Y.: Doubleday, 1958), 43.

[3]Althaus, *Theology of Martin Luther,* 118.

[4]Ibid., 119.

[5]Ibid.

[6]Wolters, *Creation,* 19.

[7]Watson, *Body,* 80.

[8]Ibid.

[9]Wolters, *Creation,* 37.

[10]Ibid.

[11]Garrett, *Systematic,* 300.

[12]Wolters, *Creation,* 42.

[13]This critique of gnosticism as a type of religion is developed in Philip Lee's *Against the Protestant Gnostics* (Oxford: Oxford University Press, 1987).

[14]Jonathan Edwards, "A Dissertation Concerning the End for Which God Created the World," in *The Works of Jonathan Edwards* (Edinburgh: Banner of Truth Trust, 1974), 1:120.

[15]James Houston, *I Believe in the Creator* (London: Hodder and Stoughton, 1978), 214.

[16]Quoted in ibid., 215.

[17]Ibid.

Chapter Six/Providence: Huck and Jim Meet Their Author

[1]Erickson, *Christian,* 346.

[2]Louis Berkhof, *Systematic Theology* (London: Banner of Truth Trust, 1969), 175.

[3]*New Dictionary of Theology,* ed. by Sinclair Ferguson and David Wright (Downers Grove, Ill.: InterVarsity Press, 1988), 541.

[4]Edwards, *Works,* 1:617.

[5]Berkhof, *Systematic,* 170.

[6]Donald Guthrie, *New Testament Theology* (Downers Grove, Ill.: InterVarsity Press, 1981), 80.

[7] Berkhof, *Systematic,* 171.

[8] Watson, *Body,* 86.

[9] Paul Little, *Know Why You Believe* (Downers Grove, Ill.: InterVarsity Press, 1969), 88.

[10] Erickson, *Christian,* 432.

[11] John Stott, *The Cross of Christ* (Downers Grove, Ill.: InterVarsity Press, 1986), 331.

[12] Ibid., 330-31.

[13] Quoted in ibid., 331.

[14] Quoted in ibid., 336-7.

[15] Milne, *Know,* 88.

[16] Ibid.

[17] Edwards, 1:616.

[18] Robert Shaw, *The Reformed Faith: An Exposition of the Westminster Confession* (Inverness: Christian Focus Publications, n.d.; orig. 1845), 72.

[19] Quoted in Piper, *Pleasures,* 63.

Chapter Seven/Humanity and Sin: Ratty, Mole and the Magic Flute

[1] *Book of Confessions.*

[2] Erickson, *Christian,* 513.

[3] Leslie Stevenson, *Seven Theories of Human Nature* (New York: Oxford University Press, 1987), 47.

[4] Ranald Macaulay and Jerram Barrs, *Being Human: The Nature of Spiritual Experience* (Downers Grove, Ill.: InterVarsity Press, 1978), 14.

[5] Ibid.

[6] Ibid., 15.

[7] Erickson, *Christian,* 537.

[8] Berkhof, *Systematic,* 232.

[9] Piper, *Pleasures,* 162.

[10] Quoted in Althaus, *Theology of Martin Luther,* 147.

[11] Ibid.

[12] Luther used the term inherited sin (*Erbsuende*) "because we have not committed it but bring it with us from our parents." On Luther's teaching regarding original sin see ibid., 157.

[13] Both Guthrie in his *New Testament Theology,* 211, and C. E. B. Cranfield in his *Romans* (Edinburgh: T. & T. Clark, 1975), 1:278-79, reject the federal headship view. They hold that corrupt nature has been passed on, but that guilt and condemnation come from our own acts of sin and not Adam's. What about the death of infants? one might ask. Cranfield denies that the passage in Romans 5 applies to infants but without adequate reasons. The view taken here is discussed in detail by John Murray in his *The Imputation of Adam's Sin* (Grand Rapids: Eerdmans, 1959), 6.

[14] The concept of common grace is found clearly in Calvin: "But if the Lord has willed that we be helped in physics, dialectic, mathematics, and other like disciplines, by the work and ministry of the ungodly, let us use this assistance. For if we neglect God's gift freely offered in these arts, we ought to suffer just punishment for our sloths. . . .

But lest anyone think a man truly blessed when he is credited with possessing great power to comprehend truth under the elements of this world, we should at once add that all this capacity to understand, with the understanding that follows upon it, is an unstable and transitory thing in God's sight, when a solid foundation of truth does not underlie it" (*Institutes of the Christian Religion* 2. 2. 16).

[15]Wolters, *Creation,* 45.

[16]Herman Ridderbos, *Paul: An Outline of His Theology* (Grand Rapids: Eerdmans, 1975), 91.

[17]Quoted in Walker Percy, *Lost in the Cosmos* (New York: Farrar, Straus & Giroux, 1983), 179.

Chapter Eight/Redemption: The Insect

[1]Quoted in Wolters, *Creation,* 10.

[2]John Murray, *Redemption Accomplished and Applied* (Grand Rapids: Eerdmans, 1955), 22.

[3]Ibid., 24.

[4]Ibid., 32.

[5]Milne, *Know,* 182.

[6]Lewis, *A Mind Awake,* 130.

[7]J. P. Baker, "Union with Christ," in *New Dictionary of Theology,* ed. Sinclair Ferguson and David Wright (Downers Grove, Ill.: InterVarsity Press, 1988).

[8]J. B. Lightfoot, *The Epistle of St. Paul to the Galatians* (Grand Rapids: Zondervan, 1971, reprint), 119.

[9]Quoted in Alister McGrath, *Roots That Refresh: A Celebration of Reformation Spirituality* (London: Hodder and Stoughton, 1991).

[10]James Buchanan, *The Doctrine of Justification* (Edinburgh: Banner of Truth Trust, 1961; orig. 1867), 17.

[11]John Brown, *An Exposition of the Epistle to the Galatians* (Marshalton, Del.: Sovereign Grace Publishers, 1970), 92.

[12]Ibid.

[13]Ibid.

[14]The reader should note that this emphasis on the future value of justification by faith is in opposition to a growing tendency in Pauline scholarship to see justification as an initial gift of God but final judgment as based on our own works. One can see this teaching in the writings of E. P. Sanders (*Paul and Palestinian Judaism* [Philadelphia: Fortress, 1977] and *Paul, the Law and the Jewish People* [Philadelphia: Fortress, 1983]). More recently James D. G. Dunn has followed this lead (cf. *Jesus, Paul and the Law: Studies in Mark and Galatians* [Louisville, Ky.: Westminster/Knox, 1990]). For responsible answers to these attempts to redefine (some might say undermine) the doctrine of justification by faith cf. P. T. O'Brien, "Justification in Paul: Some Crucial Issues in the Last Few Decades," in *Right with God: Justification in the Bible and in the World,* ed. D. A. Carson (Grand Rapids: Baker, 1992), 69-95, and Moisés Silva, "The Law and Christianity: Dunn's New Synthesis," *Westminster Theological Journal*

[15]53 (1991): 339-53.

Milne, *Know,* 189.

[16]Ibid.

[17]Watson, *Body,* 168.

[18]The discussion on Romans 6 is based on the comments of Cranfield, *Romans,* 1: 299-300.

[19]Ibid., 300.

[20]Ibid.

[21]Note the fine discussion of this concept in McGrath, *Roots,* 124-33.

[22]Quoted in ibid., 125.

[23]Jonathan Edwards, quoted in ibid., 133.

[24]Jonathan Edwards, *Charity and Its Fruits* (Edinburgh: Banner of Truth Trust, 1969; orig. 1852), 342.

[25]Ibid., 335, 338.

[26]Ibid., 340.

For Further Reading

H. Bavinck, *Our Reasonable Faith* (Grand Rapids: Baker, 1977).

James M. Boice, *Foundations of the Christian Faith* (Downers Grove, Ill.: InterVarsity Press, 1986).

Henri Blocher, *In the Beginning* (Downers Grove, Ill.: InterVarsity Press, 1984).

John Calvin, *Institutes of the Christian Religion* (Philadelphia: Westminster, 1975).

Millard Erickson, *Christian Theology* (Grand Rapids: Baker, 1985).

John Frame, *The Doctrine of the Knowledge of God* (Phillipsburg, N.J.: Presbyterian and Reformed, 1987).

Alister McGrath, *Bridge-Building* (Leicester, England: Inter-Varsity Press, 1992).

Alister McGrath, *The Mystery of the Cross* (Grand Rapids: Zondervan, 1988).

Alister McGrath, *Roots That Refresh* (London: Hodder and Stoughton, 1992).

Bruce Milne, *Know the Truth* (Downers Grove, Ill.: InterVarsity Press, 1984).

J. I. Packer, *Fundamentalism and the Word of God* (Grand Rapids: Eerdmans, 1967).

J. I. Packer, *Knowing God* (Downers Grove, Ill.: InterVarsity Press, 1973).

John Piper, *Desiring God* (Portland: Multnomah, 1986).

John Piper, *The Pleasure of God* (Portland: Multnomah, 1991).

James Sire, *The Universe Next Door* (Downers Grove, Ill.: InterVarsity Press, 1976).

John Stott, *The Contemporary Christian* (Downers Grove, Ill.: InterVarsity Press, 1992).

John Stott, *The Cross of Christ* (Downers Grove, Ill.: InterVarsity Press, 1986).

Cornelius Van Til, *Defense of the Faith* (Phillipsburg, N.J.: Presbyterian and Reformed, 1979).

B. Walsh and J. R. Middleton, *The Transforming Vision* (Downers Grove, Ill.: InterVarsity Press, 1984).

Thomas Watson, *A Body of Divinity* (London: Banner of Truth, 1970).

Albert Wolters, *Creation Regained* (Grand Rapids: Eerdmans, 1985).